S0-ASJ-640

Some Shaniko people shown at the Ste. Marie homestead at Thorn Hollow about 1915.

# SHANIKO PEOPLE

By
Helen Guyton Rees

**Binford & Mort**
*Thomas Binford, Publisher*

2536 S.E. Eleventh • Portland, Oregon 97202

# DEDICATED

to

The people who wrested a home from the high desert of southern Wasco County, and helped tame the wild in the pioneer community of Shaniko.

*SHANIKO PEOPLE*

Copyright © 1983 by Helen Guyton Rees

All rights reserved. No part of this book may be reproduced in any form or by any electronic or mechanical means including information storage and retrieval systems without permission in writing from the publisher, except by a reviewer who may quote brief passages in a review.

Printed in the United States of America

Library of Congress Catalog Card Number: 82-73596
ISBN: 0-8323-0414-X (hardcover); 0-8323-0415-8 (softcover)

First Edition 1983

# FOREWORD

"Shaniko"—whether it is the clearly defined syllabic sounds, the positive emphasis inherent in the consonants, or the unique name itself,—there is a memorable quality about it. One might forget the names of twenty other small towns, and still remember Shaniko. In the 1870's August Scherneckau was well known by the Indian families who spent the fruit-gathering season in the canyon below Cross Hollows. They called him Shaniko, a misproununciation which had come to be used by homesteaders and ranchers by the time a name was being sought for the new terminal town at the end of the first rail line ever to penetrate the interior of Central Oregon (completed in 1900). Built by local businessmen from Sherman County and The Dalles, the road branched from the main line on the Columbia River south at the mouth of the deep Biggs Canyon, down which a small stream had cut its way. The train followed up this stream. For 60 miles it traversed the rolling wheatlands of Sherman County, climbed 3,300 feet to high grasslands in southern Wasco County, and reached its terminal city of Shaniko.

Shaniko, now seen as a few scattered buildings located in a slight depression, is the only human landmark in sight. Dwarfed by the distance, it first appears as a handful of jacks might, tossed on the floor of the great plateau.

Unique in the intense individuality of the people who have lived in and around the community, Shaniko stands apart from other towns. The persons who settled and remained hailed from ten states and seven foreign countries, each bringing customs and attitudes of his own. Amazingly, during the early years, this collage of characters lived together in cooperation and sometimes even in harmony.

If the memory of these varied lives was not to slide into oblivion, it had to be recorded; otherwise, all that would be known of the unique town of Shaniko and the people who made it what it was would be the movie-type version of a small town in the wild west. With the cooperation of over fifty families, this work presents a more complete picture of the life in Shaniko during its vigorous years.

# APPRECIATION

Writing the book *Shaniko People* has been a more light-hearted undertaking because I've been spurred on by numerous expressions of encouragement: "We're so glad you are writing Shaniko history." "The book tells more about the place than you could ever know, even if you lived there. It takes you to the Shaniko of the past." "The scene is familiar, the place remains, but the people can be found only in the book."

The help of good friends who have trusted me with their pictures, told their family stories and anecdotes and answered questions was the foundation of the whole work. Thank you. And thanks to the numerous people who helped in many other ways:

C.W. Altermatt, Bertha Berg, Lottie Borthwick, Alida Brown, Madge Brown, Mr. & Mrs. Leo Butcher, Pink Butler, Elinor (Kiskila) Califf, Elyse Clark, Mrs. Clarence Ellis, Amos Fine, Mr. & Mrs. Dave Gastman, Gayle Hahn, Celia Hays, Harry Hill, Agnes Hinkle, Bob Hinton, Clarence Hunt, Elman Jones, Mr. & Mrs. Tommy Jones, John Joyce, Margaret Kimsey, Ethel Kinney, Ernest Kramer, Ed Martin, Helen McMennamin, the Rev. Dick Morgan, Mary Morgan, Ivan Olsen, Andy H. Patjens,

Lulu Paullus, the Rev. Louis Perkins, John and Teresa Reeder, Ralph Reeder, Adelbert Rees, Harry Rees, James Adelbert Rees, James & Irma Rees, Jack Rees, Alice Roberts, Pat Rose, Frances Schilling, Doris Sias, Chatty Silvertooth, Sonny Spalinger, Elizabeth Spires, Glade and Vergil Steinmetz, Lois Steward, Paul & Thelma Stoutt, Mr. & Mrs. Frank Wagner, Julia Wakerlig, George Ward, Eugene Werner, Sue Widmark, Cora Willich, Van Woodside.

H.G.R.

# CONTENTS

# INTRODUCTION

All the wealth of historical material gathered during the writing of *Shaniko: From Wool Capital to Ghost Town* and the visits with friends and "early-timers" to the area reveal much about what they did and how they lived. Without exception these people have encouraged the writing of Shaniko history, and their memories have enabled me to present it with more perception.

The work was not begun a day too soon, as time is running out for those who can give a first-hand account of their life in the busy early days. *Shaniko People* is about those who lived in Central Oregon at and shortly after the turn of the century.

In 1900-1905 the townspeople were involved in providing services to an agrarian, surrounding community of vast proportions where sheep, cattle, and wheat were waiting for market, and the new rail line was the first transportation system for 20,000 square miles of Oregon's interior.

Located 75 miles south of The Dalles, Shaniko is now seen from a distance, as though the wind-battered buildings had been tossed out like jacks on the bunchgrass prairie. Traffic speeds through what is left of town in less than two minutes, making it hard to imagine that anything of importance ever could have happened here. But for over twenty years this so-called "Ghost Town" has attracted visitors who roam around the streets and buildings, capturing in imagination what this one-time "Wool Capital of the World" was like at the turn of the century when wool was the King of Fibers and buyers came from Boston and San Francisco to bid on the best clips of wool sheared in this prime wool-producing section of the country.

In the 1870's a stage stop at Cross Hollows just over the brow of the hill from the present town of Shaniko was a busy place, supplying the needs of wagon trains bound for the gold mines at Canyon City. After the gold rush had slacked off, Elmer Lytle of The Dalles conceived the plan to build what became the Columbia Southern rail line south from the the Columbia River. The explosion of activity it brought was centered at the terminal of the line, near Cross Hollows. Vacant space near the huge warehouses was filled with wagon trains loaded with wool and supplies from as far away as Burns, Klamath Fall, and Silver Lake. Wool sales held twice a year brought bids amounting to millions of dollars a day.

The area was populated with homesteaders and small farmers at that time, so the town became a metropolitan center for their business. These immigrants and second-generation immigrants were an independent lot.

In town the newly elected city council hastened to set guidelines concerning the use and sale of alcohol and of prostitution. Elmer Lytle and the city fathers expected the community to become a place to live and rear their families, as well as to carry on their business activities. The early residents were primarily business people from established communities. They set the social patterns of the new town. The people living out on the hills and in the canyons determined their own. There was humor to lighten the times, for Dick Kinney and Bill Rees were connoisseurs of jokes. Gus Reeder represented the law to several generations of youth. The early sheepmen such as Wakerlig and Hinton tamed the prairie with vast flocks of sheep.

But all of this changed with a new rail line up the Deschutes River, the building of good roads and highways, and the use of trucks instead of rails to haul freight.

Now there are none of the early residents left. There may be twenty persons (including children) occupying livable houses in Shaniko. People still stop and peer into the windows of the vacant Shaniko Hotel and the museum buildings across the street. The Post Office is still doing business. But over the "flat" the same blue dome of sky arches over bunchgrass and sage just as it did in the beginning, and the purple hills continue their ringed guard around the horizon. If we are to recapture the Shaniko that was, it will be through the eyes of the old-timers who have shared their memories with us.

# 1

## SHANIKO PEOPLE

### "Ah, Shaniko!....Remember When"....

The 20th Century and the City of Shaniko share a common beginning, but while the latter years of the century have yet to be spent, the time has run out for Shaniko.

Thousands of people came and went during the first years, leaving their imprint on the personality of the town. Their successors, over 50 of them, have recalled incidents of the past 80 years which round out the statistics with the pulsing life of the past. Their stories deal with the Early Times, life in the small rural community, homesteading, and coping with the extremes of weather. They remember the sounds of coyotes, the fear of snakes, their youthful escapades, and their freedom to enjoy the vast, surrounding countryside. Their thoughts are shaped by the expanse of blue sky and the purple of distant hills presided over by the snow-white peak of Mt. Hood. Even their nostalgic memories reflect a kind of relief that they survived some of the rigors of the times and the adversities they encountered.

If there could be such a thing as a combined memory of Shaniko in the first 10 years, it might begin with the trip from the main rail line to the fast developing "wool capital":

In early September, 30 people step off the train and enter the depot at Biggs Junction, 20 miles east of The Dalles, Oregon, to settle down for two or three hours to wait on the hard benches lining the walls of the waiting room, until the Columbia Southern coach is ready to load passengers for Shaniko.

1

Soon some of the men begin fanning themselves with hats held in sweaty hands made gritty by the fine dust that the east wind has whipped up from the sand dunes along the upper banks of the Columbia River. Women wipe the red faces of their children and try to keep the little ones from running outside in the hot sun. Between duties, the station agent swats flies with a newspaper. For the tenth time in the hour, Zenas Moody, a portly, well-dressed man, grasps the heavy gold chain dangling across his well-rounded vest and pulls a large watch from the pocket. The hours drag by. He wonders how work is progressing on the Shaniko warehouse he is building. The Moody warehouse is well established in The Dalles, and the former governor of Oregon has every reason to expect even greater returns from his investment in the new community.

Outside, several young men, little more than boys, squat on haunches or lean against the depot wall while they exchange bits of talk about their chance of getting work on one of the ranches at the end of the line. They have just left Beaverton, North Portland and Molalla.

The train is finally ready to load passengers and people crowd up the steps and down the aisle to find seats in the comfortable, if warm, coach. The drummers stow their sample cases overhead and begin an easy conversation among themselves. The voices of some men up front drift back, snatches of which can be understood—"Homestead, Agency Plains, Bakeoven, and Ashwood" (places beyond Shaniko).

Across the aisle sits a plainly dressed young woman, looking out the window. Ada Bell is on her way to Bakeoven to teach her third term in the rural school eight miles west of Shaniko. She is anxiously wondering if there will be someone there to meet her. The first time she went to Bakeoven as a 16-year-old teacher, no one came until the following morning and she had been embarrassed that she had no money to pay for her night's lodging...

The stockmen stow their cowboy hats on the rack, cross

their legs, and strike matches on their boots to light up brown, hand-rolled cigarettes.

The train starts with a lurch, then enters the Columbia Southern tracks and starts up the deep gorge, engine puffing and laboring around one bend after another until it reaches the town of Wasco. There is a 15-minute stop for exchange of passengers, mail, baggage, and express before the journey is resumed. Similar stops are made at Moro, Grass Valley, and Kent, in addition to brief delays at a number of the 12 whistle-stops between towns. When the Sherman-Wasco County line is crossed, the wheat country is left behind and the road grade steepens again. Emerging from Kelsay Canyon, the passengers notice the hills are covered with sagebrush, rockscabs, and bunchgrass.

Finally the train whistles at a road crossing a half-mile north of Shaniko and at 5:20 p.m. comes to a stop at the end of the line, in front of the depot. Several people are waiting on the platform. The depot agent, Mr. Smith, wheels the baggage cart into place, and as people from the train pass, he speaks to the men and tips his hat to the ladies. Young Harry Hill runs up breathless to pick up a bundle of *Oregonians*, then hurries off on his route.

The women and children have gathered up bags, hats, and toys, and are soon on their way to homes a few blocks away. In the open space near the depot a buggy and several wagons are drawn up waiting to pick up ranchers from out of town. The hack Ada Bell hopes to see waiting is not in sight.

A rancher from Burns goes directly to the livery stable nearby, and as soon as his horse is ready, he heads out on his long journey, anxious to get home. He will eat and spend the night in Antelope; even then, he has several long days' ride before he reaches Burns. (As Bill Rees wrote to his father in Wales, "These Yankees think nothing of riding 100 miles on horseback.")

The drummers head down the street to one of the saloons, expecting to see someone they know and learn what's been going on in their absence. The young boys stop to inquire of waiting wagon-drivers if they know anyone needing a ranch hand.

J.W. Hoech, his wife, and several other people hurry up 4th Street to Cornett's Stage Depot between F and E Streets to make travel arrangements for Bend. They are told the stage leaves at six o'clock from the Columbia Southern Hotel a half block west as well as from Hotel Shaniko a block farther south on E Street.

The Hoech party hurries on to Columbia Southern Hotel hoping to get dinner before stage time, only to be told the dining room will not open until six, so they wait, trying to forget their hunger, until the stage picks them up.

All night long the coach bumps and sways along in the dark. At six the next morning when the horses are reined in at Bend, the famished, bone-weary young people step down to hunt a place to eat breakfast before the men go to locate the timber land they came to see. Passengers going on to Klamath Falls, Silver Lake, or Burns have more weary days of travel ahead of them.

In addition to the large Randall & Baker Livery Stable near Cornett's, there are rigs, horses, or wagons for rent at Del Howell's large stable at the west end of 4th Street. Nearby are extensive fenced holding-pens for sheep or cattle waiting to be shipped out on the train.

Fourth Street is the main thoroughfare. From the depot west to Columbia Southern Hotel (now Shaniko Hotel) is a block, and from there to Pease & Mays large department store, another. Between these large buildings are the post office, drugstore, Sanford's Store, and some small shops. Farther south a few houses skirt these blocks and four small buildings face the tracks. There are high board fences around them; these are thought of as the red-light district.

The main residential part of town is north and west, including the cupola-topped school/community hall. West of the hall looms the large, elevated box-like water tower.

After the train is unloaded, it switches the cars on the Y

and the engine is taken to the roundhouse beyond the big warehouse.

When the young teacher, Ada Bell, finds no one there to meet her she goes to the Columbia Southern Hotel. It is getting late so she registers at the long desk in the lobby, but is too bashful to linger among strangers, so climbs the stairs to her room, eats the remainder of her lunch, and goes early to bed.

In the morning she is wakened by a chorus of bleating sheep moving down 4th Street like an undulating woolly blanket; they fill the roadway between the hotel and the shops across the street. The commands of the herder and the short bark of his sheep dog punctuate their passage and nudge the animals along, directing their flow toward the stockyards across the tracks from the depot.

Outside Ada's door she hears people going down the hallway and descending the stairs for breakfast, in the nicely appointed dining room, before they leave town on the 8:20 a.m. train. In the well-filled room they are seated by Liilie McHargue, a comely young, woman in starched white apron (she was later to know Ada Bell very well, but at this time they had not met. When the children of both women had grown, Lillie McHargue Rees's eldest son was to marry Ada Bell Guyton's younger daughter).

By 10 o'clock Ada hears the creaking of heavily loaded wheat wagons, some drawn by six-, some by eight-horse teams. Soon there is a string of wagons waiting in the space near the warehouse for their turn to unload. The three Bills—Bill Mersinger, Bill Johnson, and Bill Wornstaff, aided by Tom Payne—lift the tightly packed gunny sacks of wheat from the wagons onto hand trucks. Frank Wagner weighs them, then the trucks are pushed through the large, open doors of the warehouse. The men pile the sacks 10 to 20 high in neat squares so each man's wheat can easily be identified...

Looking the other direction up 4th Street, Ada sees several teams tied to the hitching post in front of Pease & Mays store. Their drivers will pickup orders for a load of supplies, enough for several weeks or months, from the wide range of merchandise handled in the fine department store. Dick Kinney and Tom Gavin move quickly to gather up the hardware, drygoods, and clothing listed on the order.

As the hours wear on, the wind picks up dust from the heavily traveled street so the doors and windows have to be closed to keep it from settling inside...

Mary Wakerlig arrives from Bakeoven and waits outside until Ada hurries down to climb in the hack beside her. She explains the hack broke down the afternoon before, but everything is fixed now, and she slaps the reins on the rumps of the horses and they head out of town. Mary drives with easy skill. She has been riding and handling horses all her life. She is only three years older than Ada. The girls know each other well, since Ada lived awhile in the Wakerlig home last year. The younger Wakerlig children were her students.

Mary asks if Ada is still bashful as ever, "You were scared of your own shadow when you first came," she said. "Remember when you scattered the turkeys in the orchard?" Ada remembered! In fact, she had written about the episode in her diary, entitling it "Adventure in the Orchard":

## Adventure in the Orchard

Bakeoven, June 6, 1900. Very early in the morning: I am too worried to go back to sleep. Yesterday evening after the lamps were lighted, it wasn't very dark outside I thought, "I'll take a little run and get some fresh air." As usual, I ran down in the orchard. The grass made such a nice, soft green carpet, I remembered how I used to roll down hills in the grass when I was a child; I'm not very far removed from childhood now; and the more I thought of it the more I wanted to lie down in that soft grass and roll down the gentle slope.

I tied my apron over my head so as not to lose my

hairpins, took a look around to make sure the family was all in the house and that none of them were looking out windows or peeping around a corner; I lay down and commenced to roll. How nice it seemed, and what fun!

But, alas! My pleasure was short-lived; it happened that the old hen with small turkeys had found a nice roosting place under a bunch of tall grass. I don't see how I was to know that she was there, and it did seem unfortunate that I rolled down just in that place. I had rolled over but a few times, when "Auck, squawk," went something almost under me and I sat up in time to see small turkeys scattering like chaff in a whirlwind.

I thought they might go back, so went to the house and to bed, but I couldn't help worrying about those little turkeys, afraid they would die if they didn't get back. Well, this morning just about daylight, I was awakened by cries of a little turkey. I looked out the window, could see nothing, so lay down again, and thought there might be others farther away crying. The cries continued, and when I could stand it no longer (thinking everyone was asleep) I got up, slipped my dress-skirt over my gown, threw my cape around my shoulders, slowly opened the door and crept softly downstairs.

I had got the downstairs door partly opened when I thought I heard someone getting up, so I crept back to bed and listened to those mournful cries of that poor little forsaken turkey.

At last the cries ceased and I wondered if its cries were hushed forever. Later I looked out the window and saw the hen and four or five little turkeys in the yard. I *do* hope the rest are all right.

June 7. I was surprised this morning when Mrs. Alden told me she had been awake since before 4

o'clock. After breakfast I saw her feeding the turkeys
and asked how many there should be. She told me they
were all there. I counted. Now it all seems funny but
if I try to roll downhill again, I shall make sure there
are no turkeys in my path.

## Sister Cities of Antelope and Shaniko

Antelope is older than Shaniko; the two towns might even
be termed "sister cities" because of their long relationship of
business, travel, and church associations.

The wagon road from Sherman County paralleled the
railroad track as it entered Shaniko along F Street and
passed the depot, to turn right on 4th Street. At 4th and C
Streets the road turned left, going south and skirting the canyon at Cross Hollows. It passed over three miles of rising
ground before descending into Antelope, down a steep,
winding grade, taxing the holding power of the screeching
brakes and pressing the horses' breeches hard against
their rumps.

Passing the length of Antelope's main street, the road then
forked. The traveler had a choice of going east to Burnt
Ranch and eventually to Canyon City, or taking the south
fork through Antelope Valley to Hay Creek and on to
Madras and Bend. The road crossed Antelope Creek at the
lower end of the valley then it ran into Hay Creek. Before
a bridge was built, it was necessary to ford the stream, causing wagons (and later, cars) to bounce over the rocky bottom,
splashing water in all directions—if the stream was not
actually too swollen to ford.

Howard Maupin was the earliest settler in the Antelope
country. He built a cabin on the site of the Antelope that
existed in the 1860's, two miles east of the present community. He was followed by Nathan W. Wallace in the early
1870's. The old town of Antelope actually came into existence in 1873 with the establishment of a stage station at

the place Maupin first built his cabin on the pack trail leading from The Dalles to Canyon City gold mines. Nathan Wallace officiated as host at the stage station and became Antelope's first postmaster.

In 1881 the town moved to its present location. B.F. Laughlin and Nathan Baird had homesteaded the land on either side of the present main street and their common border became the main road running through Antelope. (Laughlin was later to become one of the original officers of Shaniko's Townsite Company, and an investor in the corporation that built the warehouses and developed the planned City of Shaniko.)

Little more activity took place at Antelope until 1887, the year Willaim Farr moved the old Scherneckau store at Cross Hollows to Antelope and set up his business there.

It was in the summer of 1896 that the citizens of Antelope petitioned Wasco County Court to vote on the question of incorporation, saying there were 170 inhabitants within the proposed boundaries. In October, 1896, a canvass of votes cast for incorporation showed 33 for, 14 against. The first meeting of the council was held November 18, 1896.

At the close of 1897 the town had two large general merchandise stores owned by Bolton & Company and Frank Irvine; a drug store owned by a physician and surgeon, Dr. R.J. Pilkington; two blacksmith shops owned by Peter A. Kircheiner and Antone Nelson; and three saloons owned by F.S. Silvertooth, McLennan & McBeth, and McKay & Tunny. There were four large and well-furnished hotels operated by W.J. Ashby, W. Wallace, McLennan & McBeth, and Mrs. M.E. Perrin, and a barber shop and confectionery store owned by G.E. Patterson. There were two large livery stables run by W.J. Ashby and Henry Dyce, a harness and saddlery establishment by C.F. Perrin, and a meat market by G.E. Patterson, in addition to the Antelope *Herald* printing office with M.E. Miller as editor and proprietor, there was a furniture and undertaking store run by

E.J. Glisan. Also, E.C. Dickson was building a bowling
alley and J.T. Bennett a stationery store and post-office
building. There were six fraternal societies, churches holding
services, a Christian Temperance Union (W.C.T.U.), and
various other business houses.

Monday July 11, 1898, at 2:30 a.m., a fire started in the
bowling alley and the town was awakened by cries of "Fire!"
In less than 90 minutes the business portion of Antelope was
in ruins. Fortunately, few homes were destroyed. By September many of the buildings had been rebuilt with even
better structures than before.

A good gravity-flow water system was built in 1898, supplying the city with plenty of pure water. Fire-fighting
equipment eased the anxiety of the people about another
such conflagration.

The very next year, 1899, the almost-forgotten stage stop
at Cross Hollows was in the headlines of *The Dalles Times-
Mountaineer*, date line September 20. The article stated:
"There is no longer any doubt that the Columbia-Southern
will be pushed on south from Moro to the town of Shaniko
(Cross Hollows) as rapidly as possible, and that the latter
place will for years to come be the terminus of the railroad,
for when the road is completed there will be little reason for
building farther; it will be in a position to handle all the
freight traffic for many miles south, and so long as Shaniko
is the southern terminus, it will be a lively and thriving
place."

When this news reached Antelope, eight miles away, there
were those who believed the growing town of Antelope
would "fade away." On the contrary, Antelope became more
prosperous than ever, because of the increase in population and
traffic in the area. Perhaps because of the interest of
Laughlin and Farr in both communities, the ground-work
was prepared for cooperation in their common undertakings
and the two towns never engaged in rivalries such as those
that were taken for granted between Sherman County towns

and Shaniko—which outshone them all for ten years. Perhaps the problems of isolation and the rigors of weather dwarfed and made unimportant their differences.

The founders and business people who filled the hotels and strained the available residences set about to make this the biggest commercial center in all Eastern Oregon. The minutes of the first council meetings made it clear that they expected their town to be a place where decent people would want to live and rear their families.

Abuse in the sale and use of alcohol, the establishment of bawdy houses, and the problem of gambling had to be dealt with. It was one of the first orders of business at the organizational meeting of the town council, April 1, 1901. The control of lawlessness was a continuing concern, particularly during the years the rail line was being built up the Deschutes River—and again, during prohibition.

In every direction from the City of Shaniko there were canyons with few, if any, roads leading into them, which made it possible to set up stills undetected. From these stills, moonshine was peddled for miles around. But there was a continuing series of raids made by county and local officers to break up the whole bootlegging business—sometimes half-heartedly—but never abandoned—until the repeal of prohibition made it unnecessary.

The isolation afforded by these deep hollows produced an independent and sometimes recalcitrant second generation of pioneers; wild as the horses that roamed those hills and resourceful as their ancestors had been.

The business people in Shaniko arranged their social life in much the same way as it was in The Dalles or in the communities they had left behind.

# 2

## LIFE IN THE NEW TOWN

In 1900, Frank N. Hill went to Shaniko as a bookkeeper for the Shaniko Warehouse. His wife and sons Frank and Harry joined him as soon as a small house was available. Two years later young Frank went to Portland to attend high school. Harry remained in the growing town with his parents until he too had finished grade school, in 1905. During the five years that the Hills lived in Shaniko, their son Harry observed and participated in much of the goings-on around him—and remembers them well. Most of the information in this chapter is gleaned from his clear memory—when he was 88 years old—of the Shaniko he knew and the events in which he participated.

Within a year of their arrival, a larger house became available so they moved into the second place north of the water tower. The house next to them was occupied by Mayor Frank Hurlburt and his wife, with her children by a former marriage, Sidney and Lucille Hawson. Both houses were painted white with lawns and picket fences. In the backyard there was a root cellar built in a dug-out with sod over the roof to preserve the contents from freezing in the winter. It was an effecuve cooler in the summer as well.

Harry was given several hens, a rooster and some hatching eggs. When the hens wanted to sit, nests were provided and soon there were many baby chicks to care for. There were numerous coyotes around the area, and when the chickens were large enough to be let out, Harry devised a hole in the fence large enough to let the chickens out to feed in the day time, but too small for the coyotes to squeeze through at night.

A herd of sheep coming in to Cross Hollows for water and shelter.

The large herds of sheep produced "bummer" lambs. A young ewe giving first birth may not recognize her lamb, or know how to get it on its feet to follow and suckle. The ewe shown is licking and encouraging her newborn lamb to stand.

In the fall when the flies were thick on the ceiling on a cold evening, Mrs. Hill would hold a flaming newspaper under them until they dropped down dead. Harry worked to teach his pet rooster Dick to fly to the outside of the screen doors and pick off the flies waiting to come in.

Because of the large herds of sheep around Shaniko, there were a good many "bummer" lambs. If for some reason the lamb did not or could not suckle the ewe that gave it birth, the lamb had to be fed and raised by hand or it died of hunger, exposure, or predators. Seldom would a lamb be accepted by any other ewe than its mother. One lamb was all most ewes would raise, even though they frequently gave birth to twins. A first birth was not always recognized by young ewe sheep, who would sometimes walk away and leave the lamb without knowing how to get it on its feet— or encouraging it to feed. The herders could not care for these little bummers who sometimes went from ewe to ewe in their hunger, so the lambs were given to anyone who would take them to raise.

One day a young lady from a ranch nearby rode up to the Hill house on her horse and when Harry ran out, she said, "I've got something for you," and handed down a small lamb. Mrs. Hill got a red ribbon to tie around the neck of the thin, leggy creature and they named her Topsy. Like Mary's little lamb, Topsy followed Harry to school, where she chewed on the fascinators (head scarves) of some of the girls, causing Harry to be told to take her home. After that when she tried to follow him to school he would tell her to go home and she would stand and look at him, then stamp her little feet, until finally she would go home—but she'd be there waiting for him when school was out. She was allowed to follow him on his paper route.

Occasionally she would get mixed in with a band of sheep passing the house, but the red ribbon identified her and the herder would have the dogs cut her out of the herd and chase her home.

Harry went to work after school and Saturdays for Pease & Mays store. One day the first automobile to reach town stopped in front of the store. Everyone inside joined the people who gathered in the street to see this magnificent machine with all its shiny brass trim. There was no such thing as a service station. Harry felt very important when Mr. Gavin sent him to get the handtruck and bring a five-gallon can of gasoline to service the machine.

The Columbia Southern (now called the Shaniko Hotel) was the original hostelry, but in 1903 a two-story frame structure called Hotel Shaniko was built on the next corner south. The workmen hauled clean gravel from the creek at Cross Hollows for the foundation. This hotel was operated by the James McHargue family, although the eldest daughter, Lillie, was already employed as head waitress at Columbia Southern Hotel.

Later, another two-story frame building, somewhat smaller, called the Eagle Hotel, was constructed catty-cornered from Hotel Shaniko and managed as a hotel or rooming house by a Chinese.

Harry Hill took work wherever he could find it. Each year during the two days of the wool sale he carried messages to and from buyers and sellers as well as calling people to the telephone office. He was paid a dollar per day, twice what he received at Pease & Mays Store. The hotels would be full during these wool sales, and his order for *Oregonians* had to be increased from the usual 85 copies.

The educational facilities in Shaniko the first five years consisted of an eight-grade school housed in a box-shaped building with a cupola on top. There were two rooms, the one on the east used for classes, the one on the west for a meeting place. Between the two rooms was an open space and near the door the students hung their wraps. In the schoolroom a pot-bellied stove furnished heat from wood that had been cut and stored by a man the school board hired. The chairman of the board was Julius Wiley. It was up to the teacher to start the fire and keep it going or delegate the chore to some of the larger boys. She also swept and cleaned the room.

Hanging on the wall in a prominent place were two whips, one a quirt and the other a 30-inch tapering leather switch with a tassel on the end. These were used for keeping order in the room but were used with discretion as the situation demanded. The teacher didn't hesitate to trounce a student before the whole school, a fact that had a salutary effect on all the students. Some of the big boys were larger than the teacher (and nearly as old), so this corporal punishment was not felt to be oppressive. The smaller children had other kinds of punishment, but seeing what happened to the older students was enought to encourage the younger ones to watch their behavior.

Those first five years there were three teachers, Miss Smith, a relative of Frank Smith, Lillian Vreidt, who lived in town with her mother for several years, and Miss Sturgiss who married Julius Wiley. Miss Vreidt was considered by Harry Hill to be the best teacher he ever had. He thought she married a prominent Portland attorney.

One Christmas Miss Vreidt put on a celebration for the townspeople in a loft room above the post office. The stairway to reach the room was on the outside of the building and even then there were questions of whether or not the stair would hold a crowd of people going up or down. There were no casualties and the celebration was a grand success for Harry Hill, at least, as his recitation, "Just Before Christmas I'm As Good As I Can Be," was well received.

Pupils of the school were mostly from the town, but there were perhaps half a dozen from nearby ranches who would ride their horses and tie them to poles in front of the school and go out at noon to feed them. Agnes Schmidt, who lived across the canyon, drove a cart and delivered milk to her customers as she came to school.

There was little recreation in town for the single men,

who spent a good deal of time in the various saloons, including the elegant bar in the Columbia Southern Hotel. Occassionally, the tables were moved out of the dining room and there would be dancing.

Baseball was the prominent sport, so very early in the town's life a baseball diamond with bleachers was located east of the railroad tracks. A men's team challenged rival neighboring towns along the railroad line because the train made travel convenient between towns. This rivalry became quite intense and continued until autos took people in many directions for amusement.

Mr. Smith, the railroad station agent, was the father of two daughters, Norma and Marian, and two sons; the older was named Franklin. He and Harry became good Friends. At that time there were many people from the East and Mid-west passing through Shaniko on their way to the Madras area to dry farm. Mr. Smith later resigned his job to join the farmers and Franklin and Harry bid each other a sad farewell as the Smith rig pulled out of town. Little did either of them dream they would meet many years later in a bank in Portland.

Mr. McCully ordered a new cart, and when it was delivered he asked if Harry could go fishing with him to try it out. With permission, they started off and had almost reached the canyon when the cart gave a lurch and keeled over with an axle in the dirt. Mr. McCully was precise in his speech, but he let loose a torrent of profanity that would have done credit to a freighter. The nut had come off the end of the axle and although they searched a half-mile up the road, the nut was not found.

Mr. McCully saw a cabin among some junipers, so he tied the horse to the cart and they walked to the cabin. They found a man removing porcupine quills from the face of a dog. He didn't want to be interrupted so the work continued while time flew by. Finally, he agreed to see what repairs he could make to the cart. The fishing plans were scrapped as

Baseball was a favorite sport, so a baseball diamond with bleachers was located east of the RR tracks. A men's team challenged neighboring towns along the line.

it was dark by that time and the work had to be done by lantern light. A makeshift nut was put on, the cart lifted upright, and they headed for home. When it began to get dark, Mrs. Hill became frantic and sent Frank to ask Tom Gavin where Harry was. When they finally wheeled in, Frank told his brother, "You're going to get it!" But when Mrs. Hill learned all that had happened she didn't blame anyone, and Harry was spared the feared punishment.

One of their neighbors, Dell Howell, invited Harry to accompany him to Biggs (probably to Seufert's or Fleck Orchard at Rufus) to get fruit. Mrs. Hill reluctantly allowed Harry to make the long trip in the buckboard. Driving on the dirt road was so slow that it took three days each way, with night stops at Dell's friends' places—a trip that now takes less than 90 minutes in a car.

Summer days were hot with strong afternoon winds that blew dust the length of the main street, but after the spring thaw, the bottom dropped out of the streets and roads, causing wagons to mire in the mud; then it was necessary for the drivers to pry the wheels up with planks and drive out on boards.

When rabbits began destroying the stored hay in the fields, rabbit hunts were organized and townspeople would go out and shoot as many as they found. One snowy evening when the moon was bright, the Hill boys joined Tom Gavin on a rabbit hunt. To the boys it looked like a million rabbits were gathered around the haystack. The signal was given to start firing and the boys with their "22"'s and Tom with his shotgun killed about 30 rabbits in a short time. The rancher disposed of many of them (probably for dog food) and the rest were sold by the boys to a chicken farmer for five cents each.

When Harry finished grade school in 1905, the Hill family moved to Portland in order to keep both sons in school. After Harry completed his education in Portland he worked with the Bell Telephone System 41 years, was mayor of Oswego, and served in the infantry on the Mexican border in 1916. From 1917 until 1919 he was Captain of the 162nd Infantry Division in France.

He married Mary G. Borkman who was born in Waterloo, Iowa, June 14, 1916. Their children were Harry Pershing (April 27, 1928) and Mary Jane. Harry P. had a daughter, Susan Ann, married to Donald Hope. Their children are Torrel and Dawn. Mary Jane Hill married Burton C. Walker. Their children are Jeff and Sandra Lynn.

# 3

## MEMORIES OF THE TIMES

### Water

Water was not always available near the early homesteads. In a 1904 diary entry, Ada Guyton discussed the problem of having to haul water, "We get along on two barrels of water a week. I'm careful with the water, but the horses aren't." Later, she wrote, "We moved down the canyon to Will's homestead last week, and now I can use all the water I need, I only have to climb over the rock wall to the creek and dip and carry all I want." A few years later a well was dug beside the house and she only had to go outside, down the porch steps and 10 feet away was a pump! Before they left the ranch the family had the luxury of a pump in the kitchen. They pumped and carried water to the tender garden plants in the heat of the summer.

Large cedar tanks were used by some ranchers to haul water from a windmill or creek. It was emptied into a cistern near the house. Andy Patjens built his cistern on the hill so gravity flow brought running water into the kitchen.

Charley and Bertha Burg took a homestead a few miles out of Shaniko. The land was barren, without trees or water. In the heat of the summer their small daughter Annarose played in the only available shade alongside the house. One hot day Charley left the house to do farm work. Bertha heard him urgently saying, "Go back, Annarose, go back!" He found her playing beside a large coiled rattlesnake, which he killed, but they left the homestead and moved to North Portland.

Large cedar tanks were used by some ranchers to haul water from a windmill or creek. Louisa Butler and her sons "Pinkie" and "Brother Bill" wait for the tank to empty.

Gradually the homesteads were sold to ranchers who made good permanent homes in the canyons and used the waterless hills for pasture. A few of the old homestead cabins remain; some are only grotesque reminders of the struggles of their early owners to make a home on the inhospitable hills.

## Early Buildings and Community Life

At one time the Sanford Store was on a corner across the street from the Kinney house. The post office was in the store. A little later, Blondins had a store on the lower corner of that block. It burned in the 1911 fire. Blondins lived in the house later referred to as the Kinney place. They were followed by Bogarts, Overmans, Fines, Kinneys, Maud Garrett and a number of families in more recent years.

Blondie Holstrum was a bookkeeper at Pease & Mays Store. The Holstrums lived in the long house of Grandpa (F.T.) Esping, which burned down.

The Boltons of Antelope built and operated a large, general merchandise store east of the site where Gavin-Wheeler

21

Left: Gradually homesteads were sold to ranchers who lived in permanent homes in the canyons, but a few weather-beaten cabins remain. Right: Some of the remains of homestead cabins are only grotesque reminders of the great struggle of their early owners to prove up on their land.

Life on a homestead could be bleak.

Store stood in the middle years. When the Pease and Mays large new department store burned, the Boltons sold their building to them and it was moved across C Street facing east. That remained the main store in Shaniko until Ivan Olsen tore down the building in 1960. The Boltons were in business in Antelope only, from that time on.

The "Big Hall" was just east of the first post office, later the back yard of what was known as the Kinney Place. The first floor was a large auditorium; above it was a lodge hall. One election day the women served a big chicken-and-pie dinner to the public in that hall. Mrs. Gus Reeder was in charge of the food and she furnished all the chickens. Other women brought pies and the rest of the dinner—Price 25c.

The City Band gave concerts in the Big Hall. Lillie Rees said, "The baby got fussy before the concert was over, and since Bill had to remain to play in the band, I got ready to go home alone. I felt safe. I wasn't afraid to go home alone at night but Bill Moody accompanied me home to help with the baby." (This was in 1905 when Shaniko was considered to be very wild.)

City news items copied from *Shaniko Leader* of August 28, 1902 give a glimpse of the comings and goings at that time:

> Eight or ten wagon loads of wool arrived in Shaniko from Dayville and Paulina Monday.

> A.S. Phillips started for Upper Deschutes Country last Friday with a party of "timber lookers."

> Mrs. Richard Dove and daughter, Marie, went to The Dalles to Buffalo Bill's Wild West Show.

> Mrs. Fred Wilson and mother, Mrs. Story, were passengers on the northbound train.

> J.W. Jones filed on a homestead near Agency Plains.

> Thomas Hennighan went to the Buffalo Bill's Wild West Show to gain some pointers on riding bucking bronchos.

> Visitors of Mrs. Wm. Holder were Mrs. S.S. Hays of

Moro and Mr. and Mrs. A.E. Hammond, guests from Portland.

A.O. Meyer returned to the Fatherland. A fairhaired lady had been left behind who retained possession of that gentleman's affections. When he returns, Mrs. Meyer will accompany him.

D.A. Howell family: August 23, a baby girl. Dell isn't saying anything about it, but we can see he is about the proudest papa in Shaniko.

The Great Hewett gave a fairly good exhibition to a small audience in Shaniko Monday. His tricks on the boys were good and made much laughter. His daughter, Bessie, is a clever little actress.

## Runaway Horses

Rose and Solomon Hauser remember their first day at Bake-oven School in 1898 because their parents came to pick them up after school. They were at the top of the canyon leading to their home, when the horses got scared and started to run. One of the lines broke and their stepfather could not control the horses, so he jumped out of the hack, thinking he could catch the bridle and stop them. When this failed, their mother said for the children to jump out, and they did, even though the horses were running very fast. Then she threw the baby out, hoping he would land in the sagebrush to break his fall, and she jumped too. She knew that if the hack turned over on one of them it would cause serious injury. The horses ran down over the canyon. Fortunately the tongue stuck in the steep bank of the grade, and that stopped them. No one was hurt, not even the baby.

## Scattered Anecdotes

One evening the fire bell rang. Everyone rushed to the City Hall and took the hose cart to the nearest fire hydrant, hooked up the hose and turned on the water, only to discover that the hydrant was frozen and they could not get any water. They stood and watched the house burn to the ground. It was customary to call Gus Reeder, who started the pump so there would be plenty of water, but this winter day that was no help.

The pharmacist, "Doc" C.P. Wilson, used to pull peoples' teeth when they were in great pain, since there was no dentist in town. He did not do fillings.

Nelia McLellan lived in the Rees home while attending seventh and eighth grades in Shaniko. Anna Kelly was the teacher. There were several Italian men who worked on the section crew. They wanted to learn English, so Anna had them come to her house and she taught them. Nelia had been working on her assignments at home during the day, then going to Miss Kelly's in the evening to have her work examined and graded. When her father heard about those men going there too, he came and took her home. He didn't think it was proper for her to go to that house where the men were coming in the evening.

Nelia thought it scary but fascinating to watch Lillie Rees pour hot water between the cracks in the sidewalk to drive out the rattlesnakes, then kill them with a pitchfork; it was one way to keep the snake population from increasing.

Pete Robertson, the part-Irish Scotsman, sometimes showed up at local dances. After a few drinks the exuberant Irish in him was in the ascendancy, and he was seen to grab a broom and with it as partner, dance around the room among other couples, emitting an occasional whoop.

# 4

## SHANIKO ALBUM I

Community Picnic at Thorn Hollow, 2 miles west of Shaniko, 1912 or '13.

The first four grades of Shaniko School, taught by Miss Louise Rintoul, when the Shaniko School building was new. Left to right, front row: Flossie Sumner, Adelbert Rees, Arthur Schmidt, (?), Cal Sumner, Clifford Whealy.
Row 2: Marjorie Wilson, Blanche Bentley, Elma Reeder, (?), Kenneth Payne.
Row 3: (?).
Row 4: (?), (?), Dorothy Rosenbaum, Donna Rosenbaum, Elsie Reeder, Ted Esping.
Row 5: Otto Gregory, (?), Miss Louise Rintoul, (?).

Shaniko School, fall of 1913. Lower steps, left to right: Opal Feldman, Margaret Rees, Helen Overman, Gerald Johnson, Harold Payne, Harry Rees, Lavonne Seifert, Clifford Whealy.
Row 3: Lenore Esping, Ina Page, Mary Overman, Nellie Gott, Elma Reeder, Ronald Payne.
Row 4: Morris Esping, Pierre Whealy, Arthur Schmidt, Welsley Dickey, Ted Esping, Kenneth Payne, Adelbert Rees.
Row 5: Elsie Reeder, Ruth Whealy, Anna Kelly (teacher), Frances Cook (teacher), Ernest Schmidt, and Marcus Plaster.

Shaniko School about 1912. Front row, left to right: (?), (?), Marjorie Wilson, Flossie Sumner, Cal Sumner, Morris Esping, Fred Reeder (son of Mike Reeder), Arthur Schmidt.
Row 2: (?), Elma Reeder, Isabel Coe, Marguerite Kellam, Harry Gregory, Kenneth Payne, Reams boy, (?).
Row 3: Elsie Reeder, Beatrice Reams, Dorothy Rosenbaum, Blanche Bentley.
Row 4: Otto Gregory, Miss Louise Rintoul (teacher), Donna Rosenbaum, Frank Lamborn, Pierre Whealy, (?) Reams, Jim Patton, (?) Gregory.

27

Upper left: Mary A. Ewing taught grades 5-8. Lower left: Kathryn Schueler and Alice Olsen. Right: Marjorie Wilson, daughter of an early depot agent started school in Shaniko.

Shaniko School lower grades, 1914. Front row, left to right: Harry Rees, Opal Feldman.
Row 2: Helen Overman, Margaret Rees, Nellie Gott, Tressa Magee, Agnes Feldman.
Row 3: Adelbert Rees, Gerald Johnson, Harold Payne, Elma Reeder, Lavonne Seifert, Ina Page, Beulah Esping.
Row 4: Miss Frances Cook (Rice), Clifford Whealy, Welsley Dickey, Pierre Whealy, Morris Esping, Kenneth Payne, Ronald Payne.

Volleyball Team, 1925. Front from left: Edith Hanna, Genevieve Hunt, Crystal Wagonblast, Hilda Norval, Alma Hall. Back: Gertrude Doering, Pearl Adams, Lucille Schmidt, Lottie Stephens.

Shaniko-Antelope football team, left to right: Jim Rees, Jack Rees, John Reeder, Raymond Olsen, John Reilly, Harvey Wolfe, Ralph Reeder, Lloyd Beymer, Jody Ritner, Ted McGreer, Glea Johnson and L.V. Broughton was principal.

Baseball Team, 1922. Front row, right to left: Ivan Olsen, Clifford Miller, Clifford "Fat" McCorkle, Willis Brittain, Frank Fisk, Harry Rees. Back row: Clarence Fisk, Adelbert Rees, Clyde Bonney (teacher), Fred Miller, Henry McGreer.

# 5

## SCHOOL AND CHURCH

### School Memories

During the years Frank Brumbaugh was Wasco County Superintendent he came annually and spent a whole day with the students at Shaniko, giving the student body gathered in assembly, problems to be worked in their heads. The students loved it and looked forward to his visits.

Eunice Johnson came from The Dalles in October, 1941, to teach at Shaniko. School was late starting as a result of the board not finding a teacher. Eunice had just returned from a trip to Washington, D.C. and other historic places. Among the students that year were John and Jimmy McKinley, Margaret Fine, Pat McCulloch, Margaret Olsen and Bill Rees, and perhaps two or three others. Eunice agreed to take the five-year-old Dick Rees for afternoon kindergarten classes. The older children helped Dick grow a gumdrop-tree. The teacher gave him a gumdrop to plant in a flower pot which the older students had filled with dirt. After he went home they decorated a branched twig with gumdrops and put it in the pot for him to find the next day. He was sure it grew overnight. All the students enjoyed treats for several days from the gumdrop tree.

The 4H clubs furnished outside activity for students, almost all of whom were in the fifth grade. They held meetings with other 4H clubs in nearby towns. Amusements in good weather centered around the swings in the school yard.

## Schoolteachers

The following list of teachers in the Shaniko School is incomplete, but it is hoped that the names mentioned may bring back memories of school days to the readers:

Miss Smith
Rojinia Campbell (Hunt)
Lillian Vreidt
Miss Sturgiss
Selma Johnson
Louise Rintoul
Anna Kelly
Frances Cook
Harriet Bailes
Mary Ewing
Ruth Neilson
Lola Barr
Rainey P. Burkhead
Alice T. Canning
Irene Haskins
Mary Rice
Florence Winterstein
Leafie Craig
Allen H. Pratt
Celia McCorkle
Schultes Slyter
Charles B. Roe
Clyde T. Bonney
Zella Buzan

A.N. Arnold
Mrs. John Reid
Bessie Guyton
Eunice Harris
L.V. Broughton
Lynn Hampton
C.L. Coffee
Virginia Cram (Hallock)
Jennie Hetlestater
　(Mayfield, Coffee)
Glea Sias
Maud Joynt
Arlene Estes
Velma Bichsell
Helen Rumbaugh
Eunice Johnson
Glade Carrigan
Grace May Zevely
Myrtle Ryden

## Sunday School

In addition to services of the Episcopal Church, there were occasional evangelical services conducted by missionaries of other denominations. A regular Sunday School was staffed for many years just by Christian members of the community. Mr. F.T. Esping, a Methodist, was superintendent of this school a number of years around 1915; he was assisted by some of the parents of children participating. There were years when the David C. Cook materials were in use.

Mrs. C.A. Fisk taught after Mr. Esping was gone. For several years, preceding 1929, Mr. Raleigh Casebolt served as superintendent of the Sunday School. About 1950 Mr. Francis Sutton came from The Dalles and was helped by Maud Garrett, holding evangelical services as well as classes for children. By local subscription, this group installed new front doors for the school building.

## Missionary Activities in the 1960 - 1970's

While the Morellis were operating the hotel and keeping County Wards, the Community Presbyterian Church of Moro, Oregon, began visiting the residents. It was during the pastorates of the Rev. Leo Tautfest and the Rev. Dick D. Morgan and his wife, Mary. Periodically a carload of church people would go to Shaniko and hold "sing-alongs" and serve refreshments. The residents were individually "adopted" as friends, then cards were sent on birthdays and gifts at Christmas and Easter.

## The Right Rev. William Proctor Remington

Bishop Remington was elected to be the second Bishop of Eastern Oregon in 1923. Following the unorthodox Bishop Paddock, he "came to pour oil on troubled waters," in the Diocese. He concurred with and worked for the ideas and plans of the National Church. The Episcopal camp ground at Cove became a special love of Bishop Remington and under his direction it became a spiritual center of Eastern Oregon, evolving into a summer school personally supervised

Bishop and Mrs. Florence Remington brought music into the lives of people. Mrs. Remington often gave organ recitals.

by the Remingtons. Young people were encouraged to make commitments that became fruitful in their adult lives. Several Shaniko and Antelope children attended summer school at Cove; some scarcely missed a summer. Among there were Pat McCulloch, Phyllis Hanna, Margaret Olsen, and Bill Rees of Shaniko. Two young men became priests in the Episcopal Church; one of them was Bill Rees of Shaniko.

Mrs. Remington was an excellent musician who often gave organ concerts. The Remingtons brought music into the lives of those on whom they called. The children stood around the piano while the Bishop played and led them in "Old McDonald Had a Farm," usually continuing into hymns in which the family joined the children.

Since his office was in Pendleton at the extreme north of the diocese and his travels often took him to Klamath Falls at the extreme south, the Bishop usually visited at the half-way town of Shaniko on his travels, and the Rees home was his accustomed stopping place. He often went into Glade's Restaurant and visited with anyone there. Glade tells of the day the Remingtons came in during sheep shearing. Bishop

St. Timothy's guild met at the home of Belle Kimsey at Lower Antelope, about 1934. Front row, right to left: Helen Fisher, Lila Bolter, Laura Silvertooth, Helen Rees holding Bill, Margaret Olsen, Edna Rooper holding Marie Rooper, Verna May Priday in front of Lillie Rees, Sybil Kennedy and the Bolter twins. Row 2, right to left: Eva Bolter, Louise Altermatt, Eleanor Kennedy, Allie Cram, Ellen Rooper, Allie Farrell, Alma Hougan. Row 3, right to left: Thelma Reese, (?)(?)(?) Martha Bonney, Hilma Rooper, Gladys Duus, Margaret Kimsey, (?)(?)(?), Belle Kimsey, (?), Lottie Borthwick, (?) Ada Brownhill, Grandma Rooper, Nella Rhodes, Millie Pullen.

introduced himself to the men sitting at the counter saying, "I'm Bishop Remington." One of the men said, "I'm just a — — sheep herder." To which the Bishop replied, "I'm a shepherd too, and I care for my Father's sheep," and he went on to preach the sermon of the Good Shepherd. Then Mrs. Remington sang, accompanied by two sheep dogs. The episode became a church experience among people the Bishop would not otherwise have reached.

In matters of the Episcopal Church, Shaniko and Antelope were like sister congregations, sharing services of bishop or priest, often worshipping together. In about 1933 the two communities organized a ladies' guild under the guidance of Mrs. Remington. The name chosen was "St. Timothy's" since St. Paul's at The Dalles was the sponsoring body and it seemed fitting that St. Timothy be a companion of St. Paul.

Activities of St. Timothy's included making linens for St. Margaret's House and Training Center for women deacons (now obsolete since women may study for the priesthood.)

St. Timothy's Guild Valentine costume party. Below, left to right: Barbara, Janet and Lottie Borthwick, Billie Borthwick in background, Hilma Rooper, Marie Rooper, (?). Standing: Helen Rees, Alma Hastings, Grandmother Rooper, Ellen Rooper, Lillie Rees, Laura Silvertooth. Back row: Dora Glisan, Gladys Duus.

There were fund-raising bazaars, luncheons, and dances, to assist in the local church expenses. The group sponsored social gatherings and prepared supply boxes for missionaries. This period was probably the most productive time for the Episcopal Church in the history of the area.

## The Rev. John Richardson

John Richardson, born in Belfast, Ireland, came to be vicar at St. Paul's in The Dalles in 1928 from Winnipeg, Canada. When he was a curate in Winnipeg he went to rural communities by train to hold services. There was no way to notify the congregation of his visitation, so he built a fire in the church and when the people could see smoke coming from the chimney they congregated there.

As soon as Mr. Richardson and his wife Nora were settled in The Dalles, they began monthly trips to Shaniko and Antelope. He held Sunday evening services at Shaniko, called on people in town Monday morning, then went to Antelope in the afternoon to call and have evening services before driving the 75 miles back to The Dalles. The second wedding performed by John Richardson after he came to The Dalles was that of Adelbert Rees and Helen Guyton.

When asked if it wasn't discouraging to drive so far to hold church for a handful of people he responded, "Not at all, if my coming helps one person it is worth the trip"—a remark which heightened the significance of his coming.

## The Reverend Ernest Tayler

Ernest or "Ernie" Tayler, as he was called in The Dalles, was a graduate of Virginia Theological Seminary. He was accompanied by his wife Beryl and son Robert when he came as vicar to St. Paul's Episcopal Church in The Dalles. (His daughter Jane was born in The Dalles.)

At that time St. Paul's was a mission; there were only two self-supporting parishes in the Missionary District of Eastern Oregon. St. Paul's had 134 communicants, 18 in Sunday School, and one teacher besides his wife Beryl. The Depression was tightening up the flow of funds to the Church, so, to relieve the budget, Mr. Tayler helped by taking a job at a local service station pumping gasoline.

Like John Richardson before him, Mr. Tayler made regular visitations to Shaniko and Antelope. Always soft of voice, hopeful, and cheerful, he brought a freshness to his ministry and the lives of the people isolated from church services. One of his first calls in Shaniko was the occasion of christening of Richard Harry Rees.

The Depression took its toll of Episcopalians as a number of the older families in Antelope retired to The Dalles. A small mission was organized to hold services at Cross Keys with the Madras clergy conducting worship, so the calls of Mr. Tayler were concluded, and responsibility for the

The Rev. Ernest Tayler went to Shaniko and held church services. He christened Richard Harry Rees. Godmother, Marion Lord; godfather, James Rees.

Episcopal Church in the two towns was transferred to St. Mark's at Madras.

The Depression ended and eventually Mr. Tayler saw the fullfillment of his 30 years of labor as pastor when the size of the congregation and the budget enabled St. Paul's to build a new and larger Episcopal Church in The Dalles.

## Other Episcopal Clergy Serving at Shaniko & Antelope

1924: Archdeacon Goldie, 3 months at these "Unorganized missions with no property."

1925: The Rev. J.A. TenBroeck reported:

Families Shaniko Antelope
   15         15        30
Confirmed  8        21 plus 47 persons in a "correspondence SS."

1927: The Rev. Sidney W. Creasy of Pendleton in charge. 3 persons confirmed.

1920: Report of Church Army:
   Families     3     17
   Member of the Church Army: Capt. E.S. Estabrook, Worcester, Ms. Capt. A. Buchanan, Durham, England; F.W. Whitehead, Jarvis, Sussex, Eng.; G.H. Wilde, Derbyshire, Eng.

1928: A Women's Guild was organized by Mrs. Florence Remington, wife of Bishop William P. Remington.

1932: The Ven. J. Henry Thomas, Archdeacon in charge both places.

1934: The Rev. Ernest Taylor of St. Paul's, The Dalles, following The Rev. John Richardson's departure.

1942: The work at Shaniko and Antelope became associated with the small mission at Cross Keys, and still later, with St. Mark's, Madras. The Rev. Larry Ferguson and other priests there since have made regular calls in both towns. Episcopalians drove to Madras to church.

Note: In recent years no Episcopalians live in Shaniko so this service is discontinued.

# 6

## THOSE WERE THE DAYS

**1900 - 1920**

It was popular to order the latest merchandise from a Bellas Hess, Nuquents, or Meier & Frank catalog; later, Montgomery Ward and Sears & Roebuck led the field. In a week or ten days the parcel from the "Wish Book" could be expected to arrive. Those were the days when men wore celluloid collars and a Meier & Frank suit would set you back $10, or you could buy a quadruple silverplate, gold-lined shaving mug in a lined box for $2.75. Stunning ladies' suits were available for $19.98, tailored and with braid detail.

A 60-inch linen damask tablecloth sold for a top price of 85c a yard. The latest Westmoreland sewing machine with seven drawers went for $20.75, and splendid down-filled pillows covered with German-linen ticking were listed at $2.75 each.

A puff-box of china, ivory or celluloid was used by the ladies to save the combings from their long tresses. The contents of the box, referred to as "rats" were used to enhance the stylish, bouffant hairdo. Every dresser set, be it ivory or china, included a pretty puff box.

The arrival of one of these parcels made mail time an "Event."

### Remember..."Before Radio"?

Before the radio came to amuse and beguile us, people found amusement in solving conundrums or answering

Those were the days when a stunning lady's suit could be bought for $19.98, tailored and with braid detail.

The latest Westmoreland sewing machine with four drawers cost only $20.75, and children's shoes went for $1.98—not to mention the latest children's model cars for $7.00.

quizzes. Party games were an acceptable form of social communication. Almost every community had at least one person who could "declaim," give "recitations" or favorite "readings." Children learned to "speak pieces," replete with formalized gestures. The music-hungry formed bands or organized choral groups. The "stuff" out of which this form of amusement was made was plentiful in the memorabilia of the Rees and Guyton families...Why not try out some of the following puzzles on your family and friends? They may be "good as new" by now.

**Conundrums and Such**
**From an old joke magazine, name unknown**

Why is a new-born baby like a gale of wind?..... Because it
   begins with a squall.
What kind of men do women like best?...... Husband -men
What Miss is that whose company no one wants?..........
   Misfortune.
Why is a four-quart jug like a lady's side-saddle?.. Because it
   holds a gal-lon.
What is that which has neither flesh nor bone, and yet has
   four fingers and a thumb?.................. A glove.
When is butter like Irish children?..... When it is made into
   little Pats.
Why is the earth like a school blackboard?...... Because the
   children of men multiply upon the face of it.
Why is a vain young lady like a confirmed drunkard?......
   Because neither of them is satisfied with a moderate
   use of the glass.
What were the first words Adam said to Eve?............
   Nobody knows.
How is it proved that woman was created before man?.....
   Because Eve was the first maid (made).
What Christian name is spelt the same way forward and
   backward?............................. Hannah.

Why is a kiss like a rumor?...... Because it goes from mouth to mouth.

Why was the Archbishop of Canterbury like the Prince Consort?.............. Because he married the Queen.

What is the difference between ladies and clocks?...... One makes us remember time, the other makes us forget it.

Why is an emptied room like another full of married people? ............. Because there is not a single person in it.

Which is the greatest peer that England ever produced?.... Shakespeare.

What is the grandest verse in existence?....... The universe.

What is that which is full of knowledge, and yet knows nothing?............................. A bookcase.

What is that which has form without substance and size without weight?......................... a shadow.

Name me, and you break me..................... Silence.

What is that of which the common sort is the best?.... Sense

What is that which you cannot hold for ten minutes, although it is as light as a feather?........ Your breath.

What is yours, and is used by others more than yourself?.... Your name.

What does a stone become in water?................. Wet.

Why is a man who never makes a wager as bad as a gambler?.................... Because he's no bet-er.

How would you express in one word having met a doctor of medicine?....................... Metaphysician.

Why is the alphabet like the mail?....... Because it consists of letters.

Why is a person reading conundrums like a man condemned to undergo a military execution?... Because he is pretty sure to be riddled to death.

# CHILDREN'S RHYMES

The Old Lady Who Lived in a Shoe.

1
This pig went
to market:

2
This pig stayed
at home:

3
This pig had
meat:

4
This pig had
none:

5
And this pig
cried, "Wee,
wee," all the
way home.

There was an old woman who lived in a shoe,

She had so many children—such naughty ones too!
She cried, "Oh, dear me, I don't know what to do.
Who would be an old woman, and live in a shoe?"

Once ninety little fellows sat down on the floor
And lustily screamed, "We won't cry any more!"
"Then stop crying now," the old woman said,
"The noise you are making goes right through my head."

Then she gave the boys broth without any bread,
And whipped them all soundly and sent them to bed.
She scolded the girls, and said, "Don't make a noise,
Or you shall be served just the same as the boys."

## Baby Riding

This is the way the ladies ride: Tre, tre, tree.
This is the way the ladies ride: Tre, tre, tree.
This is the way the gentlemen ride: Gallop-a-gallop-a-trot!
This is the way the gentlemen ride; Gallop-a-gallop-a-trot!

This is the way the farmers ride; Hobbledy-hobbledy-hoy!

## Puzzles and Problems

### The Industrious Frog

There was a well 30 feet deep, and at the bottom a frog anxious to get out. He got up 3 feet per day, but regularly fell back 2 feet at night. How many days are required to get him out?

The frog appears to have cleared one foot per day, and at the end of 27 days he would be 27 feet up, or within 3 feet of the top. And the next day he would get out. He would therefore be 28 days getting out.

## *The Fox, Goose and Corn*

A countryman having a fox, a goose and a peck of corn, came to a river, where it so happened that he could carry but one over at a time. Now, as no two were to be left together that might destroy each other, he was at his wit's end, for says he: "Though the corn can't eat the goose, nor the goose eat the fox, yet the fox can eat the goose, and the goose eat the corn." How shall he carry them over, that they shall not destroy each other?

Let him first take over the goose, leaving the fox and the corn; then let him take over the fox and bring the goose back, then take the corn; and lastly take over the goose again.

## *The Apple Woman*

A poor woman, carrying a basket of apples, was met by three boys, the first of whom bought half of what she had, and then gave her back ten; the second boy bought a third of what remained, and gave her two; and the third bought half of what she had now left, and returned her one; after which she found she had twelve apples remaining. What number had she at first?

From the 12 remaining deduct 1, and 11 is the number she sold the last boy, which was half she had; her number at that time, therefore, was 22. From 22 deduct 2, and the remaining 20 was 2/3 of her prior stock, which was therefore 30; from 30 deduct 10, and the remaining 20 is half of her original stock; consequently she had at first, 40 apples.

## *Cats in a Room*

A room with eight corners had a cat in each corner, seven cats before each cat, and a cat on every cat's tail. What was the total of cats?...(8)

## How Old was the Lady?

An ancient lady being asked how old she was, to avoid a direct answer, said, "I have 9 children and there are 3 years between the birth of each of them; the eldest was born when I was 19 years old, which is now exactly the age of the youngest. How old was the lady?............................... (62)

## Going to St. Ives

As I was going to St. Ives, I met a man with seven wives. Each wife had seven bags. Each bag held seven cats. Each cat had seven kits. Kits, cats, bags and wives—How many were going to St. Ives?............. (One, I was going to St. Ives)

## Up the Chimney

What will not go up the chimney up or down the chimney up, but will go up the chimney down or down the chimney down?................................. (an umbrella)

# 7

## HIGH HOPES FADE AFTER 1911

When the Oregon Trunk Railroad and the Oregon Rail & Navigation Company began hauling freight up the Deschutes River,* Shaniko knew her only future was in doing business with Clarno, Ashwood, Antelope, Bakeoven, and Ridgeway. That same year of 1911 the "big fire" swept through town decimating the hotels and stores that had provided services for the many people passing through town daily.

Shaniko residents soon settled into comfortable small-town life-styles. Depot agents, railroad personnel, schoolteachers, and hotel managers, all came and went while the long-time residents carried on their business and their personal lives as they saw fit. Warehouse crews, postmaster, storekeepers, highway crews, sheepherders, visitors and families, together, kept the town fairly lively. The old-timers like Mr. Gavin, the Kinneys, Reeders, Reeses, the Moodys, Fishers, Fines, Harrises and McKinleys—and others—made up the warp of the town. Weaving through this varied color of warp was the woof of those who had less visible involvement with the everyday affairs of the city, but who, nevertheless, furnished much of the pattern and vivid color that makes up the Shaniko mystique. The second-generation Swiss, German, and Scotch immigrants, the homesteaders, and the part-time residents—those who came and went, but called Shaniko their home—were an independent breed.

---

*The final act in the battle for control of the traffic up the Deschutes River resulted in a compromise in 1935 when the Oregon Trunk granted the (by then) Union Pacific trackage rights and the Union Pacific abandoned its tracks along the east side of the river.

The dark threads in the pattern might be thought of as the bootleggers, horsethieves, and "hangers-around." They were not many in number, but their activities touched the lives of many people. There are plenty of tales of their exploits—some may even be true—but as the years have stretched out into decades, the sharp outlines fade, and what is thought to be fact may only be fiction. It is enough here just to include in our story the lives of Shaniko people gathered from many memories. Shaniko folks are best seen as people in their time and place, doing things that circumstances seemed to dictate. Since sorting out the sequences in the lives of the many people is impossible, and finding that memory is triggered by small non-time-related events and not by any chronology of days and years, the following anecdotes are told without reference to such considerations.

## A Woman's Work

"A man works from sun to sun, but a woman's work is never done," and the old saying, "Wash on Monday, Iron on Tuesday, Sew on Wednesday, Bake on Thursday, Scrub on Friday, Polish on Saturday, and Church on Sunday," pretty well describes the work routines of women in Shaniko the first 35 or 40 years. Washing was first done on a washboard with some relief, at least, for those who could afford to send linens to the Chinese laundry.

It was a great day when the first gasoline-powered Maytag washer was available—except that it was touchy about starting. Sometimes the engine refused to go at all, leaving piles of clothing lying waiting on the floor until someone could come to start the machine. Even then, the clothes had to be fed through a wringer that popped buttons off and caught unwary fingers in its vice-like grip. The wringing was attended to while the next tub of wash was running, so there was no going off to do other chores; the homemaker stood and tended the machine the whole time. Once through the wringer the wash was hung on an outside line to dry. The arid climate in Shaniko was ideal for drying clothes. There was always some breeze blowing—if not a gale—that whipped out the wrinkles.

Ironing household linens was a hot chore in the days of the sadiron. A fire was kept going in the stove, heating the whole house in the summer, as well as the all-metal iron—which was lifted from the stove with a heavy pad. The fine linens looked like new in the hands of an expert, sometimes at the expense of blistered hands. Later, a removable wooden-grip handle was used but the iron still had to be heated on the stove. In a large family, ironing sometimes took two days.

Homemade garments were commonplace. The less affluent mothers bleached flour sacks for kitchen linens and children's underclothing. Pease & Mays Store carried a large stock of fabrics including cottons, silks, and fine laces, for those with money to buy. Those who could, traveled to The Dalles or Portland to shop for the latest fashions.

Baking was a chore that took most of the day. If it wasn't bread to be baked, it was cookies, pies, cakes or sweet rolls.

Shaniko soil is clay-like. In spite of the town's advanced sidewalk system, mud tracked into the house (or the wind blew in dust.) By Friday every room needed a thorough scrubbing. The kitchen and dining room were swept daily.

Saturday was the time to wash lamp-globes and fill the kerosene lamps, polish the silver, put on fresh dresser-scarves, and change the bedding.

## Walking

Everyone walked, no matter where in town they were going. It was part of seeing a neighbor, grocery shopping, or going to the post office for the mail. Then there was reading the mail; the day after the *Cosmopolitan, American, Christian Herald,* or *Saturday Evening Post* arrived, it was likely that someone would be found running the washing machine or stirring the gravy while reading the latest installment of "Tugboat Annie" in the Post. There was a great deal of reading done. People bought, loaned, borrowed, and read a wide variety of newspapers, magazines, and books.

"Going for a walk" was a special kind of amusement. In the 1930's Helen Rees would bundle up their four children, gather up the two nieces, Pat McCulloch and Margaret Olsen, and any other children around, and they'd set off up (or down) the highway, with the youngest children in the wagon or sled and the dog Pepper wagging behind or running over the hummocks beside the road to chase birds. One bright winter day the group started down the snow-packed road to Cross Hollows, pulling the sled. Suddenly one of the children exclaimed, "Look, there's a quarter!" Then another child, "Here's a dime"—"a dollar!" The little people climbed out of the box on the sled in which they had been tucked warmly against the chill, and they began finding money in the snow too. Everyone was incredulous.

It was like having one of those dreams of sudden wealth. They continued to pick up silver and bills for a quarter of a mile. Eventually over $25 had been picked up in small change. The next day they learned that Pete Robertson had left the Pastime late the night before, thrown the unfastened money sack on the seat of his jalopy, and taken off for Antelope. Apparently the money had jiggled off the seat and fallen through cracks in the floor. The money was returned to Robertson who gave the children the silver—eight dollars—and he kept the bills.

A walk out to "the lake" in the summer was a favorite jaunt. About a mile north of town the rock crusher had opened a spring of water that filled the excavation, making a

About a mile north of town the rock crusher opened a spring of water that filled the excavation, making a small lake. It was a spa to the water-hungry children of the high desert in the late 1930's. Charles Rees.

small lake. It was a spa to the water-hungry children of that dry country.

One evening the winter snow was just right for sledding, so the young people took their sleds and headed for Cross Hollows—an ideal slope for such activity. The full moon over their heads and the fire at the bottom of the hill to warm their hands made this night-time experience one long to be remembered.

## Hitching a Ride On the Y

Some of the boys found out that by "buttering up" L.E. Fay, the watchman on the train who looked after the engine and cleaned out the coaches, they could hitch a ride around the Y. After the passengers and freight were unloaded, the engine left the coaches beside the roundhouse. At that time the engines burned coal. One of the duties of the watchman was to pitch the coal from the coal bin to the tender. Fay certainly did not object to the boys engaging in this bit of exercise for their ride.

## Living in Town

Most families living in town, or on established ranches around, raised their own fresh vegetables. There is a story of a French lady on a homestead west of town who raised onions to sell in Shaniko during the busy growing years of the city. Older children helped with weeding and bringing in the fresh vegetables from home gardens. In Shaniko the water was plentiful and good fertilizer available from various feed lots right in town, so yards and gardens flourished in spite of the short growing season. Shaniko-grown sweet peas excelled in size and fragrance.

The boys had the chore of going after the cows. It was sometimes necessary to walk miles to find and bring them home for milking. Wood or coal was to be carried in from the woodshed. Small children loved to gather eggs. One eager five-year-old went out on his own, early, to gather the eggs from the nests. He stuffed the eggs in various pockets. On the way into the kitchen the screen door slammed and struck the eggs in his back pocket, turning a happy event into a gooey disaster.

A job the older boys sought was running messenger with election returns hot off the station agent's telegraph keys to someone waiting at the pool hall who tabulated the results while townsmen stood around eager to learn who was winning the election.

The Reeder girls, Elsie and Elma, and Madge Donley went flower picking at Cross Hollows (they called it Goose Hollow). They managed to be on their way home when the horse-drawn stage from Antelope was due. The driver, Windy Mazoo (no one remembers whether he had another name), stopped the  stage to take them into Shaniko. They showed him their flowers and he said he *loved* buttercups; and the girls *loved* riding home in the stagecoach!

# 8

## WEATHER

Southern Wasco County is considered part of the high desert of Central and Eastern Oregon. The sun is bright from dawn to dusk, making the outline of distant hills appear close at hand, for the yellowing grasses reflect the brightness of sky. The air fairly sparkles—sounds are crisp and clear. Keen eyes catch the blue flash of the mountain bluebird and ears become attuned to the lilting notes of the meadowlark.

When the winter storm clouds boil up over Mt. Hood, 50 aerial miles away, you can watch the weather in the making, for there is nothing but sky between Shaniko and the mountain. There is time to call the children home or take the laundry off the line before it breaks. Then warm clothing and a good fire are not just pleasantly welcome, they are a necessity.

When fall and spring winds blow, there is no relief from their strong and constant force. Seldom are they accompanied by rain, but heavy gusts make the houses creak and shudder. These onslaughts may last five or ten days. By eight o'clock in the evening it appears that no amount of heat will adequately affect the temperature within the rooms into which so much cold air is forcing its way. The only defense is to climb into bed in good humor and sleep the night out. The wind is not to be feared; it is to be endured.

In 1932 the snow was deep and the east wind blew cold. In five days the frost reached the pipes, freezing them solid, so it was necessary to carry water from the store, one standpipe in town still running. Pans of snow sat melting on the back of the wood ranges. The coldest night registered 36 degrees below zero. When the thermometer climbed back up to zero, it seemed so warm that people began shedding their extra sweaters.

Shaniko was in the path of the hurricane which came near the last of the "dust bowl" period. One resident was trying to secure a radio antenna when the wind picked up. His wife was holding the pole upright, but she couldn't seem to hold it steady—indeed, it was very soon apparent that no one was going to hold the pole in place in that wind, so it was lowered to the ground. In less than five minutes things began blowing across town. A large section of corrugated iron roofing blew off the warehouse as the pressure inside became unequal to the outside wind pressure. Along with flying objects came silt, like fog, in the air. The hurricane continued over 24 hours, leaving dry sand, presumably from Kansas and waypoints, drifted like snow by door and window sills.

Right after Christmas in 1937 a blizzard blew in from the east and the snow covered everything. Day after day the wind blew this snow in drifts, one way and another. From December 26 until the latter part of March, Shaniko was snowbound. The only traffic to Shaniko followed the snow plows in, but in three hours the drifts would close the road again. When the thaw came, people experienced the first colds of the new year, once they were exposed from the outside. With this in mind, one can partially visualize the struggles of Phillip T. Sharp and A.W. Boyce, both caught out in severe weather without shelter.

## Phillip T. Sharp

In 1862 Sharp wound up his affairs in Grant County and started for The Dalles on horseback, near Christmas,

Shaniko was in the path of a hurricane, about 1934. Extensive damage was done to the warehouse roof and debris flew all over town.

One winter a storm blew up cold the day after Christmas and for three months the town was snowbound. The ice on the roof of the warehouse kept creeping down until the hangover measured nearly a yard.

wanting to be home with his family for the holidays. It was a severe winter with much snow. Between Bakeoven and Sherar's Bridge a blizzard came up. It was a struggle battling through the drifts of new snow, trying to follow the road. With no shelter, and a cold wind blowing, he stamped around all night in the snow trying to keep from freezing to death. At daylight he started down the grade to Sherar's. His feet were frozen, so he cut strips from the blanket with which he had covered the horse that night, and wrapped his legs to the knees. Unable to walk. He mounted his horse, but lost the road in the snowdrifts, by now several feet deep.

It was a forbidding outlook in a blinding storm. All the gulches looked the same, but which one to follow? In his aimless search, he fortunately came across a cattle corral, and from there he followed a dim trail the cattle had made to the river. Still, it took most of the day to get to Sherar's Bridge.

Mrs. Sherar was the first to see him and she said to her husband, "There comes a man with frozen feet." She immediately filled a tub with ice water and helped Mr. Sharp into a room barren of heat, placing his feet into the tub of water; this drew the frost out of his feet, leaving a scum of ice on the water! A day later he made his way to The Dalles; both horse and rider were in bad shape. The forelegs of the horse were bandaged to the knees with gunnysacks to prevent laceration by crusted snow. The horse was taken to Jim Bird's stable, where the auditorium is now. There the hoofs came off and the animal died. The treatment given by Mrs. Sherar to Mr. Sharp saved his life, although he was always troubled with his feet afterward.

## A.W. Boyce

Boyce was a pioneer to Central Oregon, who left New York about 1876 when he was 18 years old. He walked from

The Dalles to Cross Hollows. He said, "There was a stopping place there for travelers, owned and managed by a man named A. Scherneckau." From there he walked to Clarno's Ferry and had dinner with Mr. Clarno (about 20 miles). When he asked about a job, Clarno said, "Young man, I don't know what you think about it, but there are a great many more men wanting work in this country than there is work," so he walked on to a ranch called Mail Sacks Springs, near the Muddy Creek country. Here he got a job working with sheep for two Englishmen named Tarlton and Tart. He had 25c left when he got this work, but would not have had that if Mr. Clarno had charged for dinner.

He worked with sheep for two or three years (most of the time wages were $30 a month) and then he and Gus Schmidt put their savings together and bought a small band of sheep, paying part cash for them. They took them to Cherry Creek to run them, remaining partners two years, then dividing up. Boyce moved his half of the sheep to Agency Plains. This was in 1884.

His brother joined him and they bought more sheep from Scherneckau. This brought their sheep up to 2600 head, so they divided them into two bands with a herder for each band. They camped six or eight miles apart, going to a cabin near the Deschutes River to stay and keep camp supplies.

On the 13th of December, 1884, it started snowing and kept on day after day. They had no hay; at that time few stockmen raised hay because bunch grass was good and stock usually went through the winter in fair condition. After the snow was about a foot deep, Boyce walked six or eight miles down to the place where his band was and found the herder had left the sheep up near the top of the hill because of the snow. His camp was down near the river, so he stayed there overnight. In the morning they started to drive the sheep on Agency Plains where there was plenty of grass and sagebrush for them to browse on. They both started out, but Boyce soon looked back and saw the man going back to camp. He called to him to come on. He answered, "Boyce, I wouldn't go out in that snow for $50," so Boyce went on alone to try to drive the sheep into the big sagebrush. He worked several hours, but it was snowing so hard they wouldn't move, so he left them and started to walk home. He had a large, strong shepherd dog with him, following his steps. It began to get dark and the dog started to howl and refused to follow any farther.

When he had walked about two of the six miles home, he knew he could not walk that far. It was only a mile or so to the river when Chet and Frank McCorkle kept a ferry and store, so he changed his course and headed straight for this place. There was only one opening through the rimrock; it was very dark by this time and he had doubts if he could find this opening—but he was determined to jump over the cliff if he failed to find it, hoping the deep snow would keep him from being injured. He somehow went directly to this very opening and reached the store about 9 o'clock.

When spring opened, they had about 400 head of sheep left from the 2600 with which they had started the winter. The next winter they bought more sheep from Scherneckau, giving him a note to be paid with ten percent interest, the usual rate.

# 9

## WHAT DID PEOPLE DO?

The question, "What did people do in Shaniko?" has often been asked. During the first four decades of the town's history, a work week consisted of six nine-hour days for townspeople. On the farms and ranches it was "dawn-to-dark" every day with some spare time in slack seasons to repair machinery, catch up on fence building, or go fishing a few miles away at Pine Hollow or Deep Creek. The Antelope valley was once populated by large herds of small antelope, now all gone, but there were deer to be seen on the hills in early morning and at dusk.

People living in small towns and on ranches learned to be rather self-sufficient; they knew if they didn't fix it themselves, it probably wouldn't get fixed, so they learned from neighbors, if they didn't know how. Will Guyton was such a pioneer. He and his father had bought a herd of range horses, intending to break them to work and sell them throughout the Northwest. The range land became infected with mange about that time and stock began dying of this terrible skin disorder. Stockmen devised a system of dipping animals in a healing solution. Sheep were dipped to remove ticks and any other skin disorder, immediately after shearing. Will had never before seen large draft horses dipped. Nevertheless, he built a dipping vat and for several years treated his own horses and those of ranchers for miles around. Many years later he recounted the experience:

### The Guyton Dipping Vat

"We bought range horses intending to break and sell

them around the Northwest. That was the spring the mange broke out in Eastern Oregon. If it hadn't been for that we would have made good on the horses, but we lost on the big mares; a lot of them died. We tried to hand-doctor them the first year. The second spring I told Dad we'd have to give up or fix to doctor them right. We made a big vat and ran them in on a platform, dropped them down and held them in the water to soak. We had a heavy bristle brush with a long handle so we could stand above them and scrub the scabs loose while they were in the vat. Then they were lifted up and the water with lime and sulphur—which had been boiled down 'till cherry red—was drained off so there was no sediment, as it would have blinded them.

"We had a cable with a hook to pull them up with a team. We loosened the brake on the bull-wheel and as the horse went down it wound our cable on the wheel. We built the vat out of 2 x 12's and caulked it with oakum. We had studded posts 2 x 6 and 2 x 4, two feet apart around the outside. There was a stove down beside it with pipes into vats to keep the water warm; we kept a fire going all the time.

"The vat, three foot wide, held about 3,000 gallons. It had to be deep enough that the horses couldn't touch bottom, so they were swimming all the time.

"I hadn't seen this done before, but I had to figure it out. I couldn't let my horses die.

"We took four or five men to handle the outfit, and with them we could put through 100 head of horses in a day. We drove them into a corral, then into a smaller one with a chute to the platform. It took three or four days, day and night to warm the water. We hauled the water in tanks.

"At first we were catching horses and throwing them to hand-doctor them, but I hurt my arm, which later caused facial paralysis, so we had to find another way to treat them. There was a big mare, 1400 pounds, a beautiful horse; Dad, Jim Payne and I were throwing the horses. I said, 'We've been awfully lucky we haven't hurt any of them, throwing them this way.' They were wild horses, never been around people before, and they would rear and buck. Dad said, 'No, there's no danger of hurting them.' The very next one, this big mare, fell and broke her hind leg and we had to shoot her. I sure hated to see her go. She would have made a wonderful work horse. Those horses were fighting for their lives. They would kick and fight so hard they'd sometimes bruise up their joints and hoofs until they were never so pretty again. This was during the actual dipping.

"We dipped for ourselves and other people two years—the second dipping cured them.

"After we bought the horses from Macken, Dad and I gathered 320 head the first roundup, from John Day River on the east to Deschutes River, west, and from Antelope north to Grass Valley. Macken's brand was JM. There were so many people that had JM horses that I got to using A/ brand on the hip.

"The longest trip we made was up in Washington. The year before we'd had poor luck selling around Portland. We had a sale at Beaverton and shipped the rest on the boat from The Dalles. After the Kelso sale we went up the Cowlitz River to the coast, selling wherever we could. Dad made two trips to Seattle and Tacoma.

"On one trip we loaded on the train and shipped stuff we'd broke during the winter—this was before the spring ride.

"Lou Jackson had helped us break English Cavalry horses and work horses. They were sold to someone at Baker who had a contract to buy for the Boar War. When I said they'd got cheap horses for $35 to $40 a head, he said, "No, half of them never got there. It was so hot in the hold they died and were pitched overboard." He claimed that horses from in and around Shaniko and Wasco County stood shipping better than from any other place they bought them.

"You had to keep riding all the time to keep colts branded before someone else slapped a brand on them." Guyton's cowboy days ended with the sale of the horses. He then turned to homesteading and wheat farming.

## The Train Served the People

Gus Schilling fired one of the first locomotives through Sherman County. In 1918 - 1920 the family had no transportation but a team and wagon. When one of the children needed to be taken to the doctor at Grass Valley, Gus arranged with the engineer, Otto Hinkle, to stop the train near his home and pick up his wife and child. To signal the train to stop, Mrs. Schilling stood in the middle of the track waving her out stretched arms up and down like a semaphore. The engineer acknowledged her signal with a toot-toot-t-t, and she would step off the track and wait for the train to stop. On their return they were let off at their milepost about 4:15 p.m.

Children rode the train unattended to the fair in Moro, or to school in Kent. It was fun plumping themselves down on the plush seats and waving to their friends out the window. When the train stopped in town, almost everyone was there to share in the excitement of unloading boxes and passengers and watching the loading and departure of the train with its hiss of steam then the loud sound of *choo-choo-choo* increasing in speed and finally fading away in the distance.

## And Then There Are Horses

One Sunday the Rees family spent the heat of the day in the cool canyon. When they started home the small children were tired—too tired to go another step! Their parents wondered how they would get the five exhausted little people up the steep hill. Finally, Bill Rees cut a stick horse for each child and, as his wife related, "They all galloped most of the way home."

## And Cars

Bullfrog Brown had a seven-passenger Studebaker touring car which he enlarged to haul more people—the first inter-city bus plying from The Dalles to Bend. Walter Lang drove the bus in the 1920's.

## City Sports in the 1930's

There was a good dirt tennis court beside Gavin-Wheeler Store, but the problem was the short season, since it was unusable except in dry weather. Basketball was played in the barley-roller warehouse next to the baseball diamond. Since there was no heat, only the brave or foolhardy ventured out to watch a game in cold weather. Gasoline lanterns furnished the light. About 1933-34 baseball was again popular when Shaniko and Antelope joined forces and entered the Sherman County League play-offs, attaining the championship in 1934. They had the best hitting team in the league, winning most games by lopsided scores such as 17 - 0, 30 - 3 and 28 - 1.

"As I remember," said Paul Stoutt, "some of the players were Lacoe Green, Wayne Hill, Dolph Kimsey, Bud Malone, Art, Ted, and Walt McGreer, John Reeder, Jim Rees, Paul Stoutt, Ivan Olsen, and Lloyd Troth. Ted McGreer was catcher until one Saturday night at a dance in Fossil he sustained a badly mangled thumb during activities of the young blood outside the dance hall. After that Ivan Olsen was catcher."

When the League season was over, an All-League Team was chosen to play teams from other leagues. Four players were chosen from Shaniko, and they played very well. In those days Sunday was Baseball Day, and many people packed a lunch and went with the team. Paul Stoutt told of hitting a home run. When he got home an elderly man came over, saying, "I won some money on that hit." He handed Paul a dime, which was graciously accepted, since money was hard to come by just then during the Depression.

# 10

## WAKERLIG SAGA

Among the students taught by Ada Bell were several children from the Henry Wakerlig family. Wakerlig and his wife had come to southern Wasco County in 1884 from Switzerland, via Canada. When they stepped down from the train in The Dalles with their five children he didn't have enough money to pay drayage on his baggage. By his honesty and hard work he had accumulated several bands of sheep by late 1890's and had built a substantial house at a place he called Ochoco near Bakeoven.

The eldest of the Wakerlig children, Mary, lived in the Shaniko vicinity much of her life. She got little schooling since she was needed at home to help with the smaller children; there were 11 children born to Henry and Maria Wakerlig. Mary attended afternoon sessions of school at Antelope for a short time. She married and had a daughter, Louise Young, while she was living near Bakeoven. After the end of that marriage she married Al McKinley, who had worked at Bakeoven for her father. They hads four sons, Elgin, Eldo, Bill, and Eddie.

For many years the Wakerlig family and allied familes of McKinley, Spalinger, Logan, and Lang, lived around Shaniko and Bakeoven. Mary's only daughter, Louise Young, married William Oscar Butler. They named their first son Walter Thomas, but "Pink" or "Pinkie" was the name commonly used. Their younger son, Andrew Archie, they affectionately called "Brother Bill."

Louise died while the boys were small and they went to live with Mary on the homestead. Not long afterward,

Mary Wakerlig had a daughter, Louisa Young, and four sons after she married Al McKinley —Louisa, Elgin, Eldo, and Bill. Eddie was born later.

Louisa Young married Oscar Butler. She is shown here with her son "Pinkie" and her brother Bill McKinley, who rode in rodeos and fairs around Central Oregon.

Brother Bill died of a lung infection. Then Oscar Butler took Pink and moved to Tennessee, where he left him with his mother and went to find work. Times got hard and sometimes Pink was hungry. When Mary learned this she went to work as a chambermaid in a hotel in Bend to earn money to bring him back to Oregon. After buying his ticket there was $2.70 left for the four days' and three nights' trip to Oregon. The conductor must have passed the word along that this teenager didn't have enough money. At any rate, he was met in Denver by a ladies' committee who showed him around the city during his eight-hour wait, then gave him a basket of food that lasted to Oregon. He weighed 98 pounds and said. "I was empty clear to my toes. My Uncle Ed Wakerlig took me to his place and put on an extra frying pan of food just for me. Mary got me a horse, and later, a car. She was always good to help anyone who needed it."

## Children of Mary and Al McKinley

*Elgin* and wife, Lenore, moved to Yamhill, Oregon, with their sons, John and James, and daughter, Louise.

*Eldo* served in World War II SeaBees. He married and lived at Bend. One time he was reading about the people who drink too much and decided he was a drunkard, so changed his life style. He herded sheep and worked around Central Oregon before his marriage.

*Bill* married Leona; their daughters Gloria and Lorena performed in the talent show "Stars of Tomorrow" in Portland. Bill worked in the shipyards until his death. Then Leona took the girls to Hollywood.

*Eddie* married Ruby Goff. Their children, Gene and Ramona, went to school for a time in Shaniko. Later, they moved to Independence, Oregon. Ramona lives there; Gene went to California to finish schooling. He is a medical doctor.

A well-known rodeo performer, Lorena Trickey, lived a few miles from Mary's place and was often at her home, since she was a friend of Eddie's. One of the stunts that made her famous was riding two horses at the same time, one foot on the back of each. These were not circus horses; she trained them herself. "Shaniko Red" also lived nearby and they, along with the McKinley boys, trained horses for rodeo events. Red was a prize-winning "bulldogger," having won the world championship one year in Pendleton.

Bill McKinley rode in rodeos at fairs around the small towns of central Oregon. He did a grandstand exhibition in which a horse stood saddled and blindfolded in front of the grandstand. He would come riding another horse at a run and slip off his horse onto the back of the blindfolded one, jerking the blindfold away as he did so. The result was spectacular. The blindfolded horse, not knowing what was going on, would buck and rear as hard as he could.

The McKinley boys' father, Al, remained around Shaniko after the divorce and Mary lived on her homestead. Al liked cards and gambling.

Mary McKinley was killed in a car accident late on the night of November 24, 1934. The diary she had kept between January 1922 and March 15, 1931 was given to her grandson Pink Butler. When he learned that a history of Shaniko was being written, he offered to let the diary be used for any information it contained, and he verified the use of the following excerpts from Mary's writing. To clarify some of the names mentioned:

> Vannie—Vannie Robertson, who was living on the homestead with Mary and Eldo (called Whitey because of his blond hair); Bill (called Willie) and Eddie, the youngest of the McKinley boys.
> Minnie—Mary's youngest sister.
> Walter—Walter Lang, Minnie's husband.
> Reeder—Marshal Gus Reeder of Shaniko.
> Ben Morfitt—rode for horses and stayed with McKinleys.
> Ed Wilson—a homesteader.

John Karlin—a farmer for whom Mary worked digging
    potatoes.
Leonard Armstrong—a friend.
John Singer and Cephas Gott—neighbors.
Logans—Mary's sister Bertha married Roy Logan.
Bogart—Postmaster, also marshal at one time.

## Mary McKinley's Diary

Mary McKinley's diary began in the middle of a very cold
day in the severe winter of 1922, the year that caused the
loss of hundreds of horses, cattle and sheep throughout the
area. Tiny sketches at the top of the first page of the diary
depicted a horseman looking down upon a dead horse, with
the caption, "Buried 4 horses this month." To continue in
Mary's words, "We went to town in the sled to buy grub—
snowed again—Vannie went out to see about horses. Old
Bird was dead—Willie is out looking to see how many horses
are dead. Vannie and I went out and got three half starved
colts; it was very bad—the sorrel colt died."

For all the hardships described, the diary reflects Mary's
hand-to-hand encounter with all each day might bring. She
wasted no words. When attempting to describe something,
she used her faithful indelible pencil to sketch a scene or
enlarge on an event, including funerals, which were often
complete with floral pieces and mourners around the casket.
When a letter arrived from Eldo, her delight was reflected
in the sketching of letters with line-drawn legs running swift-
ly to her. When she wrote to him, she recorded the day with
running letters addressed "To my dear Eldo." Throughout
the book there were horses in all poses of action, carrying
riders who sometimes were thrown from their backs, sometimes chasing other riders; occasionally a gun was brandished.

Every drawing, no matter how small, was one of movement and action. Mary loved horses; in fact the whole family loved horses.

In order to keep the action moving along, dates are shown in the margin for the following diary excerpts:

## Excerpts from Mary McKinley's Diary

3-21-22    My dear Eldo left the 20th of this month. It put a dark cloud in my house and an ache in my heart. He wrote to me from Mexico telling me that he has joined the Marines, that he didn't know what else to do, that he had no money and everything went wrong with him. It sure is a hard blow for me. A year ago today we all was happy together. Eldo was over at Kasers helping "lamb" and Eddie hauled hay for Langs, and Willie was home with me, and Elgie was working at Fine's, and Louisa was at Mayer's working.

4-14-22    It is still winter, a real drift storm today.

4-23       I built a chicken house. We've been building a horse corral.

4-26       Vannie and Willie catched two horses to brake. Vannie branded a colt for me and then they went to town for grub. This was a cold day. I sent a letter to Eldo.

4-28       This is my birthday. I'm 45 years old.

5-1        I went to The Dalles to get my divorce. I went to two picture shows.

5-2        I didn't get nothing done today. The boys started to plow. I sent a letter to that lonesome Eldo.

5-10       This was a cold day, one inch of snow this morning. Willie got eight coyotes in the Rees place (bounty hunting). Louisa and Pink and Brother Bill all helped get the little coyotes out. A wagon wheel came off on the way home.

## Our House Is Burnt

5-23  Last night our homestead was burnt up and the house we are in was on fire in front and in back and the barn was burnt down. This was a terrible night, a night that can never be forgotten. We found the track of a car and the car belongs to James Cooper, but he said a man stole it and run around in it all night. Reeder came, Logans came, Langs came.

5-29  Minnie and I went to The Dalles to get a warrant out for four men, and in the evening we started for home but broke down three miles out of Wasco. A man took us to Wasco, and we stayed all night. I got very sick and had the doctor to come.

5-30  We left Wasco and got to Shaniko at noon. Reeder got F. Cook and Doc and Ottis and Amiens and is taking them to The Dalles this evening. Johnnie Karlin came. Burnt on my homestead; my house and barn and all the lumber for another barn. Burnt everything in my house. (Here she listed each article of furnishings.)

6-3  Reeder and Walter took Covey to jail for burning my house.

6-8  We went to town and bought Jones' chickens and Eddie went to Tommy Jones to haul a barn in town for Tommie. Eddie seen Pony Express riders go through Shaniko.

6-27  Mrs. R.R. Hinton was shot at five o'clock this morning. R.R. Hinton came to Shaniko early this morning and told Mr. Hoech about her death.

6-29  Willie came home and got on the black pony and it hurt him pretty bad. A woman tied his head up.

6-30  Leonard Armstrong got arrested the 30th of

June for giving an Indian moonshine. The Indian died.

7-4     We didn't go anywhere. Was too poor to go to the 4th of July celebration at Tygh Valley.

7-7     Vannie and Eddie went up to my place and got a lot of horses. We branded six colts, Louisa came over this morning and I went back with her and tried on my riding shirt. We seen a colt in the wire on Lang's fence.

7-12    John Singer and Cephus Gott came, they wanted to get a bunch of pack horses. Vannie and Eddie went over on the Antelope hill to get some horses. (Here is a quote from a clipping Mary had pasted in her book: "William and Eddie McKinley are home after taking in the roundup at Prineville. They report a good time, Willie bringing back a handsome black eye.")

10-3    Willie and Eddie went to the roundup at Prineville with Miss Trickie.

12-10   This was one more long lonesome day; nothing to do, but look at the deep snow. The house is tore up, the potatoes frozen. This is a very cold house. My little colt got the lock-jaw and will die.

12-20   I got some meat from Ed Wilson. Willie and Ben went over to Lang's and got the turkey. Willie and Ben rode, while I washed clothes. Vannie stood around with his hands in his pockets and his pockets in his pance [pants], in a five-cent house out of a nine o'clock town.

1-10-23 Well, the boys are fixing to make a lot of money. Eddie will go to town and take the Bone-Crusher (Ben Morfitt) with him. He will rassel for the gate receipts.

1-11    The boys went to town and got in a fight with the two Astons [Austin and Giles Brazeau]. Willie broke out the windshield in the car and he got a black eye. Al, he was there and stopped him a'fightin'.

1-12   I went to town on old Spot and Willie and Eddie went to town too, but had to leave again to keep from being arrested. Al and Elgie came home with me.

1-13   Willie and Eddie went to town and sure made a clean-up. They shot up the old town, run all the people under the sidewalks. Louisa and Hazel (Richardson) came out afoot.

1-14   The boys are looking for the Marshal and are ready to run as soon as they see a man that looks towards them. Al went home to Jon's (Jones) Canyon, the boys went over to Langs, and layed on their porch.

1-15   Vannie went to town to see about the shooting. Willie Don, Willie, and Eddie got on their horses and left. They eat supper at Lang's.

1-16   Reeder came out to see if he could get Willie, but he was too late, the boys are gone.

1-17   The boys have gone and everything looks blue and lonely. It is a'snowing tonight and I wonder if my boys are in out of the storm. I wish I was with them. Ben Morfitt and Vannie found the horses out [of the corral] and the fence was cut in two places.

1-18   I and Vannie went to town to see how the shooting up the town is getting along. The boys are still out on the hills.

1-19   Vannie and Ben rode after horses way over Pine Holly. Didn't find much. The boys are staying out of sight.

1-20   Vannie and Ben rode after horses all day. I kept a look out for Reeder.

2-3    Ed Wilson tried to kill Bogart, there was a dance in town and moonshine was running the whole thing. Bootleggers made money by the sack full.

2-4          Ed Wilson was arrested at noon today. Louisa and Oscar came out.

2-5          Reeder took Ed Wilson to The Dalles. The boys came home.

2-26         Mrs. Singer was buried today down at Flanigan's. This was a very stormy day. Louisa came out with her children. She rode out with Willie on the hay wagon. [Mary's diary tells about Louisa's death.]

## Louisa Young Butler

4-15-23      Louisa came up and told us news. That night her and Oscar had a rowe and Oscar went back to town and stayed all night.

4-16         Louisa shot herself in the left hand trying to unload a pistol. Oscar went after her and took her to Grass Valley to the doctor. Who sent her home.

4-17         I was up nearly all night, Louisa is very sick, her hand hurts awful bad. The boys came home, I got dinner at Louisa's.

4-18         Louisa's hand was swelling fast. Started to The Dalles. This is a cold day. Frank Wagner took us to The Dalles. They cut the arm open on Louisa, but it was very bad and her side was swelled up already. Poor Louisa was suffering awful.

4-20         Louisa was suffering all day.

4-21         Dear Louisa died at two o'clock. Willie got there one hour before she died, she knew him. Oscar and children and Eddie and Minnie was thirty minutes too late. Poor Louisa is asleep forever.

4-22         We sent Louisa up on the train and Minnie went

on the train with her. Eddie and Willie and I went with Oscar and children. Elgie and Al went with Rose's [Rose Dahl] in the truck.

4-23    We buried Louisa in Hinton's grave yard. We seen her for the last time on earth.

4-24    A year ago today I went over to Louisa's to see Brother Bill, he was sick, and today poor Louisa is in the grave and out of the world, her little boys are left behind alone. Louisa was 27 years old. She suffered until she took her last breath. Her wish was for me to keep the boys and always keep them as long as I was alive, when she left Shaniko she give it [the town] one last farewell look. She never spoke over a half dozen words all the way to The Dalles. Two hours before she died she ask me if I thought she would live, she asked me those terrible words five or six times, at last she said, "Well, I give up, I wish the end was here." She suffered until she took the last breath and when she died the last words was "Hurry, hurry."

[After Louisa's death, preparations were being made to leave Shaniko.]

6-2-23    The boys started to Redmond with the cattle and the next day everyone left in two wagons, camping on Hay Creek the first night, Box Springs the second and Crooked River the last night. By the 9th they were settled, had found a place to live, and Pink and Brother Bill seemed happy.

## Summing It All Up

Since Mary McKinley's diary reveals a great deal about the life "out on the breaks" of the canyon and perhaps "out on the

breaks" of life, considerable space has been given to her very
real description of life as she saw it. Numerous other incidents
were recounted: The family killed coyotes for the pelts and
bounty; she mentions one day that was so cold "the fire froze in
the stove, the wind never quit blowing this day."

Another time she said, "Vannie let the ax fall in the well, so
he took Eddie by the feet and let him down in the well to get
the ax out, and then he pulled him up again.

They branded colts, picked gooseberries, cut hay and rode
after horses, "to get ready to go to Denver with them." They
were plowing, seeding, fence building, well digging, trailing
horses and sheep, repairing harnesses and saddles, and making
lariats [hair ropes].

In October 1928 Mary wrote, "No one knows how dear a
homestead cabin is until he is out of a home." From then until
September 1929 Mary herded sheep in the snow and cold,
rounded up cattle, helped load the water wagon, dug potatoes,
"until I was sick and every one was little tinie potatos." Often
she would say, "I worked hard all day and never got nothing
done." She milked the cows, fixed the fence and wrote about
the wind blowing dust in her eyes until everything was covered
with dirt. In February 1931 she said, "I am lonsom for som-
thing. I want to go over the hills and canyons. If only I could
get a place and some sheep I would be happy. I sure wish I
could go on a ranch and make garden." This was while she
was working in the hotel in Bend. Eventually she and Eddie
moved back to the Shaniko country.

Mary's later years lacked the zest for living portrayed in early
1922. She was known to have said, "When I die, don't bury
me, just tie my feet to the saddle-horn, slap her on the rump,
and set her off running and dragging me until there's
nothing left."

In one period of discouragement she wrote, "This is a hard
world to live in. I worked hard every day but never get
ahead. There's no use of living when there is no freedom.
The one that's free in this world is the happiest and richest

person in this world! Without freedom, all the gold is nothing. I have looked for freedom all my life, but I am still a slave, and the road is rough and rocky as far as I can see." Somehow it seemed fitting that her death should have come suddenly and violently.

[Mary McKinley Drawings]

In her diary, when Mary McKinley wanted to describe what happened, she didn't waste words, but took her indelible pencil to sketch a scene or describe an event, including funerals which sometimes included mourners around the casket. When a letter arrived from her son, Eldo, her delight was reflected in sketches of letters with legs running to her. There were horses bucking, carrying riders who chased other riders—sometimes brandishing a gun. Every drawing, no matter how small, was one of action.

We built a horse corral

Mrs. Singer was buried
at ten o'clock this
morning

Eddie went to town but
had to leave again to
keep from being arrest-
ed.

The boys are looking
for the marshal and
are ready to run as
soon as they see a man
that looks toward them.

From my dear Eldo

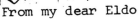

Edies homestead
caben

1929
November 1st Edie going to Shaniko

Edie going to Shaniko

Willie going to Shaniko

I'm lonely for my kids and I'm thinking
of the days when the kids and I lived
on the homestead and every Sunday they
would saddle their horses and go fishing
until dark....Deep Creek was their playground.

## Wakerlig Family

**Parents:**
**Henry Wakerlig (August 1, 1852—March 26, 1914)**
**Maria Wittwieler (May 25, 1851—February 29, 1906)**

Henry, eldest son (September 17, 1877-November 24, 1934), settled in Malheur County....Edwin "Ed" (Oct. 10, 1879-July 18, 1977) was a small child when a fall injured a hip so he couldn't walk for several years. Finally he fashioned himself a crutch from a piece of wood and learned to walk with that. When he was ten years old his sister Julia was born. It was customary in large families to encourage an older child to think of a newborn as his baby to look after when parents were busy or out of the house. Ed gladly accepted the responsibility for Julia when his mother placed the new baby in his arms and said, "Ed, she is your baby." A close bond grew up between brother and sister that lasted a lifetime. Ed would hoist the toddler up on his shoulders and with the help of his crutch, carry her around. Eventually he no longer needed the crutch, though he always had a limp.

Ed took up a homestead in the Bakeoven area and lived there much of his life. In his later years he sold out and went to Harper, Oregon, to stay with his sister Anna and her husband Johnny Medlin. He helped them and worked sometimes for other people around Harper.

After World War Two Ed lived in Boise with his sister Julia. He died there. Julia said, "When I was young, Ed looked after me, and when he was old I looked after him."

Bertha was born fourth in the Wakerlig family (January 2, 1881-January 4, 1963) before they emigrated from Switzerland. When she was twenty-one she married Roy Logan. The wedding took place at the Thomas Burgess home in The Dalles. Roy Logan had run away from home when he was fourteen years old. From Benton County he went into Washington where his older brother lived. He probably slept nights in someone's barn—then asked for a meal when he was hungry. He thought he could stay with his brother, but when he finally got there the reception was so cool that he stayed overnight and left before breakfast the next morning. He eventually made his way to Antelope, where he and Vivian Bolton got a job working together at the Hinton Ranch. Then Henry Wakerlig hired him and he met Bertha Wakerlig.

After the marriage they both worked for Newt Burgess at Antelope. Roy did ranch work and Bertha cooked year-round. Their children, Ray and Alma (Ellis), were born there.

Twins were born to the Logans, Aug. 31, 1906, and were named Margaret and Madeline. Madeline died when a small child. There was a fourth daughter born later who died in infancy.

When they had saved enough money they took up a homestead close to Bakeoven. Roy Logan raised sheep. One year he shipped sheep to Omaha, then Chicago, thinking they would bring a better price there. Each stop, the price was lower than at the last. Finally, he had to sell and took such a loss that it almost broke him. He sold out and with a thousand dollars he and Bertha started for California. (The ranch was sold to Hinton.)

In California he took a mechanics course and worked a while, then later raised almonds at Arbuckle. Bertha was talented, as were all the Wakerlig girls. She learned to paint and sold several oil paintings to Jackie Coogan.

Roy Logan died in Arbuckle when 79 years old. Bertha lived until four days after her 82nd birthday in 1963.

Rosa (January 25, 1884-November 18, 1906) lived to be only 22 years old. She died at Bakeoven about two weeks after her mother; both had typhoid fever. They were buried at the Hinton Cemetery. Rosa was engaged to marry Herb Mulkins when she became ill. Several other members of the family were very ill at that time. When Henry realized how serious the disease was, he sent the rest of the sick children to The Dalles Hospital. There were seven in all who contracted the fever. At the hospital, the rest survived. Mrs. Walter B. Brown nursed Mary Wakerlig.

Ernest (October 27, 1886-November 1, 1927) went to Westfall where his brother Henry lived, when he left Bakeoven. He was married there, but later separated from his wife, "It was so hot, there was no shelter from the heat, the water wasn't good, and she was so lonely that she went home to her family. Years later Ernest lived in Butte, Montana. He died there and was buried in Ontario, Oregon.

Julia (March 25, 1888-) married in 1904 when she was fifteen years old. There were more men than girls around Bakeoven, so the girls married while very young. Her husband, Warner Spalinger, had come from Portland. There were three girls and two boys in the family when his mother died. Warner was two years old. The father and other members of the family raised the children. Before he went to Shaniko, Warner had worked in a cracker factory owned by his uncle and for Swift & Co. slaughter house. At Bakeoven he got work with Henry Wakerlig.

The Spalingers lost their first child, a son, but raised a daughter, Pernita, born Sept. 20, 1906, and a son, Henry "Sonny," born May 16, 1908.

The marriage between Julia and Warner Spalinger ended in divorce. Julia undertook to raise the children by herself. Times were very hard for her. The children started school in Shaniko, attended a while in Bakeoven but went back to Shaniko in bad weather. Julia lived in The Dalles for a time and they attended school there.

After the children were away from home, in 1925, Julia took up a relinquished homestead near Ed Wakerlig's ranch. Julia tells of her life there:

> They said the house was on the homestead so Ed moved me down. I didn't have no light. We forgot the

coal oil and sure enough midnight it started raining. The house had four rooms. I couldn't tell which room this sound was in—it wasn't a snore, it wasn't a groan, it was just a funny thing goin' on. The little dog growled and growled and wanted outside. I couldn't sleep any so I set out there 'til it got daylight and then let the dog out. He went around the house and whined. Then he went under the house. I looked and he was dead. [The event apparently "spooked" Julia.]

The homestead adjoined that of Fred Zogg. One winter I was snowed in there, couldn't get out no way. You know my cabin was right in a narrow gorge. On one side the snow drifted clean to the roof. Fred Zogg and another fellow come with a load of wood for me. I was clear out of wood, and had tore down the partitions in the house, to burn. The day before, Fred come to my house with snow clear to the horse's breast, and he said to me, "Are you still alive?" and I said, "Yep," and he come in and I told him, I said, "I'm just about out of wood." To start in, I had 98 new posts to build the fence. I burned all of them, and then I had four rooms, and I tore all the partitions out for a fire. The next day he was out there and brought me some wood.

And then in a couple of days Sonny came and he said, "You better come go over to Ed's with me." He was afoot and I was afoot. He left first and then I started out. I told him I couldn't make it. The snow had packed and was drifted; he come back again the next afternoon to see why I didnt show up. He brought two horses. We got out then.

Ed went to school very little. He said, "there's lots of books and you can learn if you're not too crazy." Ed was good at figures. He could figger faster in his head than I could on a paper. Ed was more like a dad to me all our lives, and we were together most of our lives.

You know, I trapped coyotes. I had a trap line about eight miles long. Every day I'd go around, so a coyote wouldn't get in a trap and suffer. That was a long ways to walk. When I'd go around the trap line I'd come by Ed's place. He always had a piece of mutton or maybe a few eggs for me to take home. I never had any meat unless I could shoot a rabbit.

Pernita moved to Portland. She married Jessie C. Hopkins. He died five years later in 1941. Later, she married Charles Butts. Now, in 1980, she maintains her home in Portland.

Sonny did ranch work around Central Oregon and even worked a while in Montana. He was a good mechanic and caterpillar operator. When he retired he moved to Boise to live with his mother.

Julia worked in the shipyards and many other places during the war. She whittled horses from wood and covered them with unborn calf hide. Many of these horses were sold to patrons of Pernita's bar.

Julia, 94, lives in Boise.

Walter (July 24, 1889-January 27, 1968) was born on the Ochoco Ranch. Like others of the Wakerlig family, he went to Southeastern Oregon. He died in 1968 in Boise, Idaho.

Anna (July 16, 1891-August 27, 1952) was also born on the Ochoco Ranch. When Anna was 16 her mother died. The family had lived at Bakeoven ten years. The work of keeping up the house and cooking for so many people as well as tending store and post office required many long hours of hard work. The older girls had left home and when her mother died, Anna's father expected she would do the work just as his wife had done. It was too much for a 16 year-old girl. She told her father she was going to leave. He laughed and said, "You will never leave." She answered, "I will!" and she did.

She and her niece, Louise Young, packed the horses after the men had gone to bed, tied their clothing in a bed roll behind the saddle and left in the middle of the night. Her father was sure they would come back in a day or two. They rode all night long, headed for Westfall where her older brother Henry lived, in Malheur County. They stopped at farms along the way and asked for a place to stay and something to eat. It took them a long time to reach Westfall because Louise was sick on the way. She was not sturdy and was often sick. She was twelve. They had no money. Henry was delighted to see them. They stayed. Anna did not go back.

Henry Wakerlig gave up after she left. His kids had all left and he was there with just hired people—and Minnie. Anna married John Medlin.

R.R. Hinton was a neighbor of Henry Wakerlig. Some years after Maria Hinton died, her husband married Mary Anne Bird, a school teacher. Bishop Paddock performed the ceremony. The Bishop was a good friend of the family, sometimes spending a week with the Hintons at the Imperial Stock Ranch. R.R. would drive the Bishop to make visitations, in his Locomobile car.

Hinton and Mary Ann had two children, Mary Loula "Mary Lou" and Richard "Dickie."

Minnie Wakerlig was twelve or thirteen when her sister Anna left home. Her father worried about her because she was just a little girl, and there was no woman left at home, just hired men. Dickie Hinton would go to Bakeoven after the mail, and he liked to talk to Minnie; she was a pretty girl. He loved to tease her and would come to Bakeoven on all sorts of excuses just to see her. The two fathers talked about their children marrying some day. Dickie was a little wild, but R.R. was sure that he would settle down, and Henry wanted Minnie to be in a safe place. The two fathers arranged for Minnie to come to the Hinton ranch and be tutored along with Mary Lou. The Hinton children had never attended Bakeoven school.

Minnie was unhappy and homesick. When she was 16 she and Dickie were married at Mrs. Schenck's home in The

Dalles. The plans of the fathers didn't work out as expected. Dickie did not settle down and Minnie was not happy and secure. Dickie would disappear for weeks at a time. Finally Minnie and their son, Bobby, moved in with the Hintons. She was now eager to get out of the marriage. Finally she borrowed money from her father-in-law, left Bobby with them and went to Portland to business college. When she was about 19 she divorced Dickie, got a position in Portland and eventually paid back the money she had borrowed for her schooling.

These were stormy years for the Hintons. Mary Lou did not marry, but became mentally ill. She spent her time going from the ranch to an apartment in Portland. Finally, she was so distraught that she climbed over a barricade and jumped from an upper window of the "Wheel and Annex Apartment" where she was staying. The fall killed her.

Her mother, Mary Ann, was worried about her family and spent sleepless nights hearing Mary Lou calling her. One day when her grandson Bobby was with her she showed him a paper saying, 'I want you to go and tell your mother, today, be sure, that there is a paper in this Bible that I want her to get." Mrs. Hinton owned some land, the Buzan Place, and she wanted Bobby to have it, his mother thought. That night Mary Ann Hinton shot herself. The paper was never found.

When Mrs. Hinton was gone, Minnie quit her job in Portland and returned to Shaniko, took Bobby and went to work for Leola Loring in the telephone-post office. Later, she married Walter Lang. They lived on a homestead near Shaniko.

Henry Wakerlig sold Bakeoven Ranch to W.H. Moody shortly before World War I and retired at Westfall. He sold all his holdings and gave each of his children a thousand dollars, then left for an extended visit in Switzerland. His daughter, Anna, and grandaughter, Louise Young, went to Europe to join him. When they were ready to leave

Minnie Wakerlig and her niece, Louisa Young.

"Bobby at the Old Fishing Hole." This picture, taken by his grandmother, Mary Ann Hinton, won first prize in a *Liberty Magazine* photo contest.

Minnie Wakerlig Hinton was the first woman to drive a car across the Wapinitia Cutoff. This picture appeared in the Sunday supplement of the *Oregonian*, proclaiming the event.

Switzerland they found there would be difficulty getting tickets to the United States because of the war. They did some touring in Europe, then secured passage to England, and from there, home.

Not many months after Anna reached home, she was called back to Switzerland because of the critical illness of her father. He died before she arrived, so she returned home alone.

Dickie Hinton was coming and going to the Hinton Ranch, never staying long. The following story came from numerous sources, most of which agree on the details: Dickie was on his way home on the train. It was a trip taking several hours and he was nipping a few as he traveled. Shortly after the train left Kent he became so exuberant that he shot out the lights and windows of the coach, pulled the stop cord, and when the train slowed, he jumped off and hiked the several miles over the hills and canyons to the Imperial Ranch. It is generally believed that when the bill arrived for this dramatic "Wild West" exit from the train, it cost R.R. somewhere between $1,500 and $2,000.

# 11

## SHANIKO ALBUM II

Freight team in Shaniko 1910.

Joe Morelli collected wagons and built a wagonyard during the "Ghost Town" days.

Jim Rees bought two old Overland cars. One had a good engine, the other a fair chassis. Darrel Altermatt and Eugene Werner helped switch the good motor into the good frame, then they put a hood on both ends. When the seats faced one in each direction, it appeared the car was always going backward.

John Reeder with the highway truck in front of the City Garage, 1940.

Memorabilia on display in Shaniko Hotel - (Morelli collection).

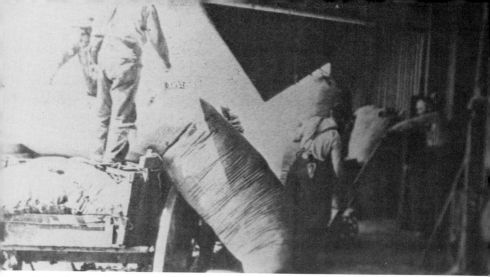

Unloading wool at the warehouse.

The piler lifts 400-pound sacks of wool to store in Moody Warehouse.

Gus Reeder's harness shop.

Loading sheep into stock cars.

# 12

## AFFAIRS IN GENERAL

### Rural Electrification

The coming of the REA line was to transform all of Eastern Oregon outside the cities. Prior to its construction, people had no electricity unless they owned one of the small Delco plants which charged heavy duty batteries. Normally, during peak hours the "plant" was kept running to prevent too great a drag on the batteries; otherwise, the electricity was used directly from them. It was impossible to use appliances requiring heat, such as hot-water heaters, irons, or stoves, but lights were a great benefit compared to coal-oil lamps, or the more brilliant light of gasoline lamps, which had to be "pumped up" and mantles changed frequently. Electric lights were considered a luxury.

Slim Carrigan, always innovative with mechanical devices, once bought a windmill and installed it to recharge his batteries, thus saving on gasoline and plant wear. It was an excellent idea, except that the windmill was not built for those Shaniko winds and soon the thing ran away with itself. Off flew the "works" and that taught Carrigan to turn the mill off when hard winds were blowing.

### Epidemics

In addition to the early smallpox and diphtheria epidemics described in the book, *Shaniko from Wool Capital to Ghost Town*, there were continuing attacks of the influenza first known in 1918.

For a number of years, onslaughts continued to occur at intervals of two or three years. On February 21, 1921, the Council met in special session with W.A. Rees as acting mayor; the group considered the advisability of having a dance at the Columbia Southern Hotel because of contagious diseases scattered throughout the county. All gatherings were prohibited until the Council decided the danger was past.

In 1930 there was a smallpox scare and the health authorities from The Dalles came to interview those who had been exposed, instructing them to be sure their immunizations were current (within the last ten years) or submit to quarantine.

This brings to mind the evidence of progress that has been made in immunization to prevent communicable diseases. In 1918 smallpox was making the rounds while the Guyton family was living in Arizona outside of Phoenix. School children were required to be immunized or be under quarantine at home. Not many parents understood the immunization efforts. Some said they didn't want serum from cows injected into the arms of their children, so kept them at home. The method was primitive, the idea novel, and it was with considerable fear that the children allowed their arms to be sandpapered until the first blood appeared, then watched as drops of serum were placed on the sore. A bandage was then applied and they were told, "Do not remove the bandage for three days." The problem was how to keep from peeking. Some had badly swollen arms, shoulder to elbow and, of course, all carried scars—or it was considered ineffective.

In 1935 The Dalles was the location of a Tuberculosis Hospital which served the surrounding counties. Periodically, Marion Lord, the county health nurse, came to the southern part of Wasco County to give school children the routine test to determine if any child had contracted the disease. One year she found between eight and ten children in Antelope and two in Shaniko who showed a positive

The Guyton Family was wintering in Arizona when the smallpox epidemic struck and the children were given vaccine serum from cows, crudely injected in their upper arm, sometimes leaving large scars.

reaction to the test. Extensive sleuthing was done to locate the source of the infection. It was learned that a young man staying in Antelope and working on a nearby ranch drank from a hydrant where school children often stopped to refresh themselves on the way home from school. The man was required to go to The Dalles to take the "TB" test. Within hours of having been given the "Patch Test," he appeared at the Health Center complaining that they had used contaminated instruments because his arm was badly swollen and was itching and hurting. This being the evidence of active "TB," he was required to enter the Tuberculosis Hospital immediately. Within a year and a half he was discharged, cured. Had the disease not been discovered, he would probably have been dead by then. (How fortunate we are to live in a generation which scarcely recognizes the symptoms of "TB," smallpox, typhoid, or measles.)

With special care, including medication, proper diet, and plenty of rest, the children soon showed negative tests, so there were no further cases. This is one of the last active cases of "TB" discovered in the area.

## Movies

Occasionally, after movies were available, one would be shown in Shaniko. Everyone in town turned out and sat on the hard benches for hours. *The Hunchback of Notre Dame* with Lon Chaney was an eleven-reel show and there was only one projector, so in addition to the showing time, there was a recess between every reel while the film was being rewound or broken sections spliced. It made quite a long show!

## Basket Socials

Basket socials were popular affairs, planned to raise money for school or Sunday School. Gus Reeder auctioned the baskets, W.A. Rees kept track of the bid, and Arch Altermatt took the money. At one social Andy Bollens was bidding on the basket of Theo Illingworth; $10 was a high bid, but the bidding went to $20, and that was as far as Andy could go. Than Cavin bid $21 and got the basket, causing great disappointment for both Theo and Andy.

Another way to raise money was the "shadow auction." A girl stood behind a sheet, casting a shadow which was visible from the audience. It was not always possible to identify the lady by her shadow, but the bidders thought they could and bid up the lady of their choice for the privilege of sitting with her and eating a delicious box lunch at her side.

Jim Rees attended one of these auctions with 55 cents in his pocket. He loaned Clarence Fisk 50 cents because he was trying to get enough money together to eat with Margaret Logan. The loan did the trick; she was his partner. When Gertrude Olsen, who was a small child, cast her shadow on the screen there was an awkward pause with no bidding, so Jim bid his remaining 5 cents and had a nice lunch with little Miss Olsen.

## Two-way Overland

Jim Rees bought two old Overland cars. One had a good engine, the other a fair chassis. Darrel Altermatt and Eugene Werner helped switch the good motor into the good frame (cost $12.50). The car had a self-starter, but Jim usually cranked it for lack of a good battery. The little car was beautiful to start in any weather. The gas tank was under the hood, so a little awkward to fill. In fact, the whole car seemed a bit clumsy, since the boys put a hood on each end, making it appear the car was traveling backward, no matter which way it was going. Jim drove it to Barkerville, B.C., to visit his Uncle Robert Rees, who was operating a gold mine by hydraulics. There was no windshield or top, and since it rained a good part of the way, it was a damp ride.

During the trip the Overland developed several problems—among them a leaky radiator which Jim took off and mended, a broken front spring which he replaced at a junk yard, and clutch failure which required professional help.

He arrived, hoped to find a nugget or two, fished, and finally started home. He had just made it across the International Border at Blaine, Washington, when the car gave up entirely. He found a buyer with five dollars' cash, kissed the old chassis goodbye and loaded his belongings, including a beautiful set of moose horns his uncle had given him, onto the train and finished his journey.

When the Rees house seemed too small for the growing family, Adelbert built a tent house on the lot to the south where some relative of Cornet lived before the fire. Some time later, he moved to the warehouse watchman's room so the insurance rules could be satisfied; and Harry Rees tore out the frame and built a house for himself. His father gave him old lumber from the warehouse with which to work. Before long Jack was building his own house, too, next to Harry's. The boys lived in their cabins until they moved away from home.

## Fiddlers Three

Amos Fine was a young fiddler when Les Holt was an old hand at playing for dances. Les was a good fiddler, but he sometimes drank too much and didn't last the evening out. Amos remembered one Saturday night when Les played only part of the evening. It was customary to take a collection for the musicians and when the fiddlers were paid off, Les got one dollar and the other fellows got two. The next week Les asked why he was paid less than the other musicians. If he had been told, "Les, you got drunk and quit early," everything would have been okay. However, he was told, "The musicians all got the same." Les knew better and he hit the manager of the dances, knocking him out into the darkness—and the fight was on. Les pulled out his pocket knife. He cut up the man so badly that he was taken to the hospital in The Dalles and barely recovered. Les was put in jail. By the time the other man was out of the hospital and it was sure he wouldn't die, Les was released because he had served enough time for the charge of assault.

After everyone had a car, the big Saturday night dance was popular. Often there would be a dance Friday night, as well. People from all the towns attended the large dances— Shaniko, Antelope, Maupin, Tygh Valley, Kent, Grass Valley and Moro—with music furnished by an orchestra from The Dalles. Small dances usually attracted people from a smaller area such as Shaniko, Antelope, and maybe Maupin.

Couples enjoyed playing "500," and here again there was an exchange between towns. The lodges in Kent and Antelope held monthly "500" parties in their halls, with 10 to 15 tables playing for prizes. Smaller groups met in homes where bridge was often the game played.

## Indians at Shaniko

In the spring the Warm Springs Indians stopped at Glade's Restaurant to eat and to sell salmon on their return from fishing at Celilo Falls. In the autumn they came from huckleberrying. The men were served their meal first, but an older woman handled the purse for all. They were kind and uncomplaining.

Indian women and children came to the area to camp three or four days on Porcupine Ridge to dig camas (a bulb of the onion family) and gather herbs. They borrowed cream cans to carry out water for daily needs, always returning them clean.

Two of the women, Josie McCorkle and Mrs. McBride, said that before white men came the Indians met on a big sandy meadow crossed at one end by a creek. It was like a big fair ground, located on what was later part of the Jim Fisher Ranch. They called this summer camp *sim pa te*. While the tribe was camped here the women gathered roots and the men made obsidian arrowheads. When they were ready to break camp they held athletic games and competitions and raced their horses, then had Indian dances and religious ceremonies before leaving.

These women explained how they got their names McCorkle and McBride. A fire in the forest was burning all around the Indian encampment. Two priests newly arrived from Ireland helped the Indians get into the creek and put damp cloths over their faces, which saved their lives. In honor of the two priests, the different members of the group chose to be known by the name of one or the other, McCorkle or McBride. They proudly continue to be known by these names.

One of the Indians once remarked, "Shaniko is on the Reservation, but we gave it to you because *we* didn't want it!" (Boundary for the Reservation is about twenty miles west of Shaniko.)

## Hard Rocks into Hard Cash

Once it became known that there were rocks around Shaniko and Antelope that were of interest, people began carrying them home. Rockhounds came from far and near to scour the hills. Crusher sites, outcroppings, or just out on the hills, good stones waited for the seeker. One of the early collections of note was gathered by John Silvertooth of Antelope. People rigged up rock saws and tumblers to cut and polish their stones. Slim Carrigan was one of the first Shaniko residents to cut and polish stones and make jewelry—just for fun, not to sell.

It was about this time that rock mining began on Hay Creek south of Antelope. The red rock is used for facing buildings. Now visitors pay to comb the hills for rocks, pay for them by the pound, and visit the Richardson's Rock Shop on upper Hay Creek to buy rocks to add to their collections, or to purchase gift items of polished stones.

There are still discoveries to be made on the high desert of Eastern Oregon. In the 1920's there was excitement when oil drilling began in the Clarno area, and while nothing came of it, that great canyon of the John Day River may contain treasures not yet unearthed.

# 13

## SHANIKO INTERLUDE

### Vista

As the crow flies, a crow could fly from Government Camp, on the shoulder of Mt. Hood, to Shaniko without an appreciable change in elevation, for Shaniko nestles on the plateau at about the same elevation as Government Camp, with nothing but thin air between. Most of the time this thin air appears clear blue; when at its brightest it enables the traveler at the summit of the plateau west of Shaniko about 12 miles to see the crowning peaks of the Cascade Range from Northern Washington's Mt. Rainier to Central Oregon's Three Sisters. If the earth surface did not curve, the other snow-clad mountains could be seen in the distant south. This panorama of mountain peaks set against the blue of sky is best seen on a clear cold winter day or in the early spring.

In order, the mountains which may be identified are Rainier, St. Helens, Adams, Hood, Jefferson, Three-fingered Jack, Mt. Washington, the North, Middle and South Sisters of the Three Sisters group, and Broken Top. Unlike the mighty Himalayas, from which many peaks from one massive range, the Cascades display their crowns at intervals of from 10 to 30 miles. Eruptions of eons past have formed each peak with its distinctive beauty. Until recently one would have described St. Helens as "that perfect cone," but the past two years have seen her change until she, too, now has an eruption-scarred form.

The peaks mentioned are those retaining iced fields year-round, and do not include visible peaks such as Haystack, Black Butte, and Mt. Bachelor.

In the evening when the last radiance fades from behind Mt. Hood, the evening star takes its twinkling stand, then gradually surrenders its place in the nighttime sky to the constellations as they emerge framed in the marine blue dome of the heavens, then the awesome realities of great earth and boundless depth of sky dwarf the person, yet leave one with an awareness of being part of this vast and mysterious world.

### GHOST TOWN 1960

Shaniko is a ghost town? You might say so—
But my mind is aglow
With recollections borrowed and abridged,
That still cause the heart of the
Town to beat a lively pace.

There are the near-armies:
Groups, crews, gangs,
Scottish, Irish, Swedish, English and Jew.
Cowboys thundering their mounts in street races,
Sheepherders and homesteaders scraping
The bar rails with boots and high-top shoes.
(Where are those bar rails, now?)
Shots rang out often—smacked flesh seldom.
Curses split the air—shoulders hit the dust.

Blacksmiths had a busy time of it
Fitting rosy hot shoes to hooves,
Springing the new bands on wheels,
Creating parts for broken plows.
Stables were crowded with tired horseflesh.
Some had labored all the way from John Day.
Others, highly groomed, awaited a weekly foray.

The streets were peopled with drummers and dreamers.
Some found their hopes, others lost all.
If you were thirsty and broke, you could unload a dray.
A foaming mug would be your pay!
The festive time was wool auction day.

Much harder to take was the screech and grind
of the baler.

The bell rope hangs untouched by the hand
of a school marm for many years;
And the cool dark hall no more contains
the tread and dash of children's feet.
Still *I* hear them.
Lined up for a drink of water after recess;
Puffing as they pulled on galoshes
To trudge out across the knolls,
Past juniper, sage and gooseberry—
To their country homes, where evening chores awaited.

Jail cell doors have not clanged shut
On the vagrant, drunk or horse thief for four decades.
The fire bell rings louder in my mind than in reality;
When many saw the "handwriting on the wall,"
Had fires—
Collected their insurance,
And struck off for greener climes.

And the wheels! Could you count them?
Dray wheels, freight wagon wheels,
Buggy, stagecoach, spring wagon, and surrey wheels;
Churning up the mud or dust—
Carrying in the product of the land;
Wool, Hides, Barley, Oats, and Wheat.
Carrying out the needs of the scattered settlers:
Flour, Sugar, Whiskey, Gingham, Coffee, and Tea.
I can hear them. Have you counted them?

Greater still than all of these are the sounds
That no longer carry on the prairie breeze,
Like the whistle at the trestle
North of town. You'll hear it no more.
Tracks, Trestle, Depot, Round House—all gone.
Hissing steam no longer escapes as when
The black monsters halted at the station.
Blatting of sheep and bawling of calves is now silenced—
Once carried on a cloud of dust from the stockyards.
(They're gone, too.)

Graveyard? Well, I tell you
There isn't one.
Bed rock is four inches down
And dynamite wasn't *that* plentiful.
Where are they buried?
Imposed on their neighbors and laid to rest
In Antelope, or Bakeoven, where the ground is more welcoming.
No church or graveyard, but plenty of ghosts.

"How could you live in such a Godforsaken place?"
(a phrase that often fell on my ears)
Though their concern was a welcome thing,
I pitied them that they could never see
Through the veil that Time concealed,
The quick hot flash—like a prairie fire—
That was Shaniko.

Mary Ada "Pat" Rose
(abridged)


## ECHOES

Have you ever stopped to listen
For the far off tinkle of a bell
To tell of freighters coming
With loaded goods and tales to tell?

Have you ever closed your eyes
And felt the hustle, bustle
Of the rangy cowpokes horses
And the maidens silky rustle?

Have you ever felt the seeking wind
As it whistles o'er the sidewalks
To tickle hollow-eyed windows
And peek-a-boo in useless locks?

Have you ever seen the sunset
Against ghostly silhouettes below?
You'll experience all of this and more
In the little town of Shaniko.

—Sue Morelli

# 14

## SHANIKO PEOPLE AND THEIR FAMILIES

The family stories are arranged alphabetically by surnames in the belief that the threads of events will be woven into the historical design in the telling of the lives of over 50 residents of Shaniko.

Adams, John Family
Altermatt, Archer
Bonney, Clyde T.
Borthwick, Lottie Stevens
Brown, Walter B.
Bruner, Ferdinand H.
  "Farnum"
Casebolt, Raleigh
Donley, Hiram
Esping, Frederick T.
Esping, Albert T.
Fine, John E.
Fisher, James E.
Guyton, Claud Thomas
Guyton, Glade
  (McCulloch Carrigan
  Steinmetz)
Hanks, William D., Jr.
Hinton, Robert "Bobby"
Hoech. J.W.
Holt, Andrew
Keeney, James H.
Kinney, Richard E.
Kramer Family
Lord, Marion
McHargue, James J.
McKinley, Al
McLellan, Nelia
  (Kentner Bergstrom)
McLennan, John
McLennan, Duncan

Moody, William Hovey
Moody, Clara McFarland
Moody, Zenas Ferry, Governor
Moody, Mary Stephenson
Morelli, Joe and Sue
Nicholson, Millie Inman Holt
Olsen, Peder Johan
Patjens, Andrew (Andreas)
  Family
Payne, Leslie Boyce
Reeder, Children of Gus
Rees, William Arthur
Rees, Lillie May McHargue
Rees, William Adelbert
Rees, Lillian Margaret
Rees, Harry Alfred
Rees, John Robert
Rees, James Angus
Reid, John
Reinhart, Family of William
Rhodes, William E.
Rintoul, Louise
Robertson, James, Sr.
Schmidt, Children of Gus
Wagner, Frank Phillip
Ward, George
Werner, Charles and Alma
  Grossman
Whealy, Family of Samuel
Wheeler, Roy and Ida Baker
Wilson, John J.

## The John Adams Family

John and Bertha Adams came to Oregon from Indiana with their two children: Oscar, born November 8, 1893, at Cherry Tree, Pennsylvania; and Olive, "Ollie," born at Twin Hills, Indiana, January 28, 1897. John took up a homestead at Rutledge in Sherman County but abandoned it and returned east to Pennsylvania.

At that time it was common for children to sell "Mother's Salve" door to door for premiums. Oscar wanted a violin so the two Adams children accumulated enough premiums to buy a violin, Ollie was also eager to learn to play. When she was about ten she picked up the violin and learned to fiddle without lessons.

The family later returned to Oregon and John bought back the place he had homesteaded. Several years later he moved to the Bruner place just north of Shaniko. The family called it "Honneysuckle Farm" because there was honeysuckle growing there. The soil was too poor to farm so John raised cattle. He sometimes referred to the place as "The Land of Milk and Honey" though it certainly was not a "Land of Plenty."

Ollie wanted to go to high school in Kent, so got a job doing housework and sorting and washing eggs for the store in order to go to school. There were a lot of young people around Kent when she went there. They gathered for Saturday night dances in someone's home. The furniture would all be moved out of two or three rooms, the carpets rolled back, the floor waxed, and they danced until early morning to the music of the fiddle. Ollie said, "Sometimes I'd play." There would be a dance when someone laid the floor for a new barn, then neighbors brought refreshments and they danced all night.

Young Ollie Adams found joking as natural as fiddling. One time she decided to surprise Will Guyton when they were on a fishing outing by putting a dead fish in his bed. "He didn't say a word," she said, "but a few nights later I found limburger cheese in my bed." Ollie recalls:

"Among my friends were Anna Schassen, Louie Clark, and Elner Helyer. Anna and Louie got married later and so did Elner and I. We lived in the Wilcox area several years, just south of Kent. Our children were Virginia, born October 16, 1916, and the twins Bertha and Myrtle, born April 13, 1918. Then Norma Jeanne was born, January 16, 1926, and Gordon, January 1, 1934. When the children were pretty well grown we moved to The Dalles. Elner died there in June, 1973; we had celebrated our golden anniversary in 1965.

"After Anna Clark died I heard how discouraged and sad Louie was so I went to see him. I was lonesome too; Elner had been gone two years. Louie and I enjoyed each other so much. Well, I went to see him often—we decided to get married. Two years later he died, but we had those two very happy years together."

## Oscar Adams

Oscar Adams married Mary Maggie Bamer of Boisford, Washington, and lived near Kent where their first child, Doris, was born. She died in the 1918-19 influenza epidemic. Oscar never had attended a funeral until he went to the last rites for his little daughter.

Oscar first farmed at Wilcox, then around Kent. They moved to Hood River where he had an acreage and raised fox for pelts. Several years later they had a son, Leland. One time the Boy Scout troop from Hood River hiked up the Columbia River Highway and entered the Mosier Tunnel to look out over the river from the stone balcony. A landslide occurred just at that minute and Leland was killed by falling rocks. The Adams family had another son, Connie, who grew to maturity in the Hood River area.

Oscar Adams died November 8, 1966; his wife Mary died February 20, 1969.

John and Bertha Adams had a daughter born in 1910. Pearl attended school in Shaniko, then rode the train to high school in Kent, along with Mabel Holt. Pearl attended Behnke-Walker Business College in Portland before her marriage to Emmet Eakin. They had one son, Ronald. The Eakins make their home in Dallesport, Washington.

## Archer "Arch" Altermatt
## September 1886-October 11, 1945

Arch Altermatt was born in Springfield, Illinois, and grew up in Albany, Oregon, where he met his wife Louise in 1905. Louise Mildred Dalsgaard (1880-1949) was born in Evans, Minnesota. Their two sons, Darrel Dalsgaard and Robert B., were born in Albany. Arch had taken a correspondence course in art and was working as an industrial artist. He went to Shaniko as a sign painter, then his brother-in-law, Jack Fowlie, offered him a job with Eastern Oregon Banking Company. He was employed there until the Great Depression closed the doors of the bank, then he moved his family to The Dalles.

The pictures Arch painted over the next 39 years showed much talent. He was interested in portraying real western life and painted Mt. Hood, Multnomah Falls, and wagon trains crossing the Deschutes River. The latter picture now hangs in the Wasco County Court House at The Dalles. Some of his family felt he should have pursued his art as a career rather than go into banking.

In The Dalles he was in the Wasco County Tax office until World War Two, then went to Portland in 1943 to work in

Left: Arch Altermatt was working as an industrial artist when Jack Fowlie offered him a job with E.O. Banking Co. in Shaniko. Many years later when he was preparing his paintings for an art show in Portland, he died suddenly. Right: Jack and Dorothea Fowlie with Louise Altermatt and her son Darrell in 1911. Unidentified lady in background.

the shipyards. By this time his sons were grown. Both eventually settled in California.

About 1945 word was received that Arch Altermatt had prepared to show his paintings at an art show in Portland, but died suddenly of a heart attack just before the show was to have opened.

## The Altermatt Family

The Altermatt Family was originally from Switzerland. The first recorded Altermatt was Karl Altermatt von Ramiswil, married to Maria Ackerman. These parents wanted their son, John Baptist, born in 1812, to become a Roman Catholic Priest, so they sent him to Italy to study. He had ideas of his own and bypassed the studies and was disowned by his parents. In 1847 he married Dorothea Rueckert

(1831, Sachsen, Germany). When John was 25 he and Dorothea went to Sauk County, Wisconsin, where their son, Pius Fredrick was born, Feburary 13, 1848. They had ten more sons and one daughter. The family settled in Leavenworth, Minnesota, where he became a township official and postmaster.

Pius Fredrick married Bertha Sist in 1873. Bertha was from Sweden. The following children were born in Sleepy Eye, Springfield, Minnesota: Dorothea, Alphons, Gertrude, John, Mabel, Nelson, Archer, and Sidney. One daughter, Elizabeth, was born at Albany.

### Clyde T. Bonney

Clyde Bonney came from the Willamette Valley, as a boy, to Tygh Valley. The family settled on what was later known as the Bonney Gold Ranch. Augustus A. Bonney, father of Clyde, was a farmer and stockman. Bonney Meadows was named for the pasture where he took his cattle in the summer and Bonney Crossing for the place he crossed a stream en route.

The family of Augustus A. Bonney spent the school year in The Dalles while Mr. Bonney remained on the ranch. Mrs. Bonney, the former Elizabeth Jones, died in The Dalles in 1887. Clyde went on to school at the University of Oregon. He played right tackle on the first team that ever beat Oregon State College, in the late 1800's.

While in college he met his wife, Martha, of Hood River. They married and reared three children, Rex, Margaret, and Thelma B. Rex was a veteran of World War I. Margaret married Dolph D. Kimsey of Lower Antelope. Thelma married Ernest A. Reese. also of Antelope. Thelma was postmaster at Antelope for several years.

Clyde taught in schools in Central Oregon including Tygh

Valley, Shaniko, and Sisters. He became supervisor of Wasco County Schools under Mr. Neff between 1914 and 1920. In carrying out his duties to the 85 schools then operating in the county, he traveled first in a two-wheeled horse-drawn cart, then in a Model T Ford Roadster.

Clyde Bonney was principal and teacher in Shaniko from 1924-26. Probably because there were not enough students in Maupin and Tygh Valley to maintain a school, he brought 17 students from Maupin, Tygh Valley, Wapinitia, and Clarno to Shaniko and boarded them during the school week. They lived in the house Adelbert and Helen Rees later occupied (Ivan Olsen eventually moved the house to Madras). The boys slept in the Allie Brazeau house nearby. Mrs. Bonney cooked for all of them. During these years, Shaniko High School had a good baseball and football team coached by Mr. Bonney.

Following are the out-of-town students who attended high school when Mr. Bonney was principal in Shaniko:

| MAUPIN | WAPINITIA | CLARNO |
|---|---|---|
| Genevieve Hunt | Friend LuCore | Henry McGreer |
| Alma Hall | Clifford McCorkle | |
| Clifford Miller | | |
| Ira Kidder | | |

| TYGH VALLEY | | |
|---|---|---|
| Gertrude Doering | Willis Brittian | |
| Faye New | Clarence Nelson | |
| Ray New | Clifford Brown | |
| Verda Wing | Clair Norval | |
| Fred Miller | Hilda Norval | |

## Lottie Stephens Borthwick

Lottie Stephens, daughter of Elgie Stephens, was born at Burnt Ranch, July 1, 1906. Early in 1926 she moved to Shaniko to work at the hotel, owned at that time by John McLennan and operated by Matt Asher. She lived with the Clyde T. Bonneys part of a year, then with the Rees family until her marriage to Eldon Borthwick on February 26, 1927, by the Justice of the Peace at the Wasco County Courthouse. When they arrived at the courthouse they were surprised to meet neighbors they knew. Oscar and Hanna Thompson had just been married there before the Borthwicks arrived. Daughters of the Borthwicks are Barbara (Feb. 27, 1928); Janet (March 27, 1930), and Billie (October 22, 1931). Eldon has farmed at Lower Antelope many years.

## Walter B. Brown

Walter B. Brown was a pioneer farmer in the Bakeoven area. He and his wife were friends of the Wakerligs. Mrs. Brown was at Wakerligs caring for Maria and the other ill members of the family when Maria Wakerlig died.

Welsey "Slim" Carrigan was a small child when his mother came to work at a farm near the Browns. She died, leaving Slim an orphan, so the Browns raised him with their own son Andrew J.

Andrew and Alida Douma were married September 14, 1926. Their daughter, Jean Ingram Gabel, lives in Maupin. She had a daughter, Jan, and a son, Edward. Andrew sold the farm to Lee Lindley in 1972 or 1973 and retired to live at Maupin. He died about 1975.

Alida taught the Bakeoven school two years, from 1924 to

1926, and says that shortly after their marriage they cooked for the carpenters who were building the Bakeoven barn after the original one burned in 1926. Alida had sisters Anna and Adeline and twin brothers.

The blacksmith shop and hall at Bakeoven were torn down when the road was widened.

## Ferdinand H. "Farnum" Bruner

Farnum Bruner, son of German-Swiss parents Henry and Charlotte (Brunner) was born in 1863 near Racine, Wisconsin; grew up at Hardington, Nebraska, and took a homestead there, then married Melda M. Wadding in Brookfield, Pennsylvannia (born in 1877).

Farnum and Melda came to Oregon when their son Herb was an infant, and homesteaded land now known as the Adams place. Three children were born there: Ivan Raymond 1900, Oliver Wayne 1902, and Abigail 1904. The land was shallow and rocky, and Farnum was not a farmer, so he took work as section foreman for the Columbia Southern Railway Company. He owned and managed the new Hotel Shaniko for a while. Around 1905 he sold out and left Shaniko for Spokane to be foreman on the railroad there. Two more children were born there, Don F. and Ruth Genevieve, before the family moved to Arcata, Humboldt County, California. The last child, Elinor Melda, was born and grew up at Arcata.

## Raleigh Casebolt

Raleigh Casebolt was a nephew of Mrs. J.W. Hoech. He went to Shaniko from Myrtle, Missouri, to work in the

Farnum and Melda Bruner wedding picture. Farnum was not a farmer and the land on his homestead was not farm land, so he sold out and ran Hotel Shaniko, then sent for his relatives, the Woosters, from the East and they operated it, so he could take the job as section foreman for the Columbia Southern Railway Co.

Eastern Oregon Bank. He and his wife, Myrtle, had six children: Clifford, Gerald, Donald, Lillian, Wilford, and Bryce. When the bank closed its door in 1929, the Casebolts moved to Sunnyside, Washington.

## Hiram Donley
### Engineer on the Shaniko Line

Hiram Donley's father was superintendent of Bridge Building on the OWR&N Line. When his son Hiram wanted to be an engineer on a train, his father helped him get work on the Columbia Southern Railroad into Shaniko. By pre-arrangement he met his fiancee, Nona Illingworth, at her sister and brother-in-law's farm house near Kent in 1902. The ground was covered deep in snow when Hi Donley swung down from the engine and waded to the house to claim his bride. The following day the Rev. S.C. Elder of Kent performed the ceremony and the couple boarded the next train to live in Shaniko.

The picture of the train in the snow was enlarged as a 25th anniversary gift because it was taken near the spot where Hi Donley left the train to claim his bride. It is now hanging in the Shaniko Post Office.

"Helping Daddy oil up the big engine." When the engineer, Hi Donley put the train to bed, his son Gordon was his willing helper.

Left: Hi Donley, early engineer on Shaniko Line, was on the train that carried the body of Mayor Fowlie to The Dalles. Right: The Donleys had a daughter Madge and son Gordon.

Hi Donley was engineer of the train that took the body of Mayor Fowley to The Dalles.

The Donleys had a daughter Madge, born in Shaniko in 1903. Mrs. Gus Schmidt was midwife at the birth. Gordon Donley arrived in 1909, also in Shaniko.

The Donleys lived in a home near the round house, but when the red-light district was established next door, they moved to another part of town. Madge was just a tot but she remembers the high board fence that was built around the four small houses, completely enclosing them. She was fascinated to see a group of new "Pretty Ladies" (as she thought of them) get off the train in their high-plumed hats and their wasp-waisted dresses to walk from the depot to the houses. Periodically the "ladies" would leave and another group would appear on the train to take their places. "None of them ever went anywhere in town, except to the bank." said Mrs. Brown, adding: "We never had any money and our parents would not let us accept generous gifts from drunken sheepherders, but I learned to shinny under the raised board walks to look for coins they dropped when being thrown out of the saloon."

The Donleys lived in Shaniko about 14 years, then moved to Moro. Madge graduated from Emanuel School of Nursing in Portland, served in the Army Nursing Corps, and became a 1st lieutenant. She and her husband, James L. Brown, have lived in Portland many years. They were married in 1927. Gordon Donley was a graduate of Oregon State College. Gordon was also in the army. When he retired he had attained the rank of full Colonel. Gordon Donley died in 1981.

When Madge and Gordon heard a new post office was being dedicated in Shaniko they thought it a fitting place to display a large framed picture their mother had presented to her husband years earlier. The picture was an enlargement from a picture post card. A photographer named Raymond from Moro had seen and photographed the train plowing through the snow not far from the place the young Hi Donley had joined his bride-to-be.

## Frederick T. Esping

Fred Esping was born in 1848. He learned the carpenter's trade in Sweden. When he was about 15 he packed up his tools and came to America. After serving in the Civil War he went to California, then to The Dalles, Oregon, in 1884. He and his wife Olivia (1851-1897) had two sons, Albert (1877) and Harry.

Attracted by all the building being done in Shaniko, Fred

and his boys took their tools and went there. He built a number of homes, was active in school affairs, led Methodist Sunday School and church services, and even preached occasionally, though he was not an ordained minister. He was a very religious man—"No card playing! No working on Sunday" in his home.

His skill as a carpenter, his interest in the school, his leadership in religious services, and his personal life left a deep impression on the children who grew up while he lived in Shaniko.

His second wife, Clara Blaine, was a nurse working at the Hinton Ranch when they met, They left Shaniko about 1924.


## Albert T. Esping

Al Esping married Elizabeth Delcor (1878-19). In 1911 Al Esping was building a house with the help of a Mexican man from a neighboring town. It is believed, though never proved, that Al was robbed and beaten by his helper and left to die. He was found in the vicinity of Shaniko and taken to The Dalles, but never regained consciousness. His daughter, then five, remembers seeing him in the hospital with his head all bandaged. About two years after Al's death his wife and the children moved to The Dalles.

Their children were Lenore Olivia (1889-1981), Theodore (1903-1913), Morris Watson (1905-1943) and Beulah (November 10, 1907). Lenore married John Lally, October 14, 1919. Her second husband, Alfred Knudson, and she were wed in 1956. In 1964, and widowed, she married a classmate from the Shaniko days, Otto Schmidt. (He and his first wife, Esther Christiansen, had raised two sons, Robert and Roger.) Otto died in 1980, Lenore in 1981.

Theodore was drowned while learning to swim in a slough of the Columbia River, after the family moved to The Dalles.

His water-wings collapsed. His friend, Clarence Ellis, was with him.

Morris Watson Esping was killed July 25, 1943, in Australia, while serving with the Merchant Marines. He was buried in the Punch Bowl, Honolulu, Hawaii. The youngest child of Albert T. Esping, Beulah, married T. Graydon Calbreath in Vancouver, Washington, in 1927. Their daughter Jean married Fred Shaw. Graydon joined the SeaBees in 1943.

## John E. Fine

John Fine took up a homestead about ten miles from Shaniko, northwest of the Arthur Schmidt place. In 1927 he left the area "because there were getting to be too many people." He joined the Bogart family, who were on their way to the gold rush attracting people to Winnemuca, Neveda. They were traveling by wagon over rough, rocky roads when the wagon struck a large rock and the jolt threw Fine off the wagon, which ran over and killed him. His children were George, Ebenezer "Eb," and John E. Fine.

George Fine, the eldest son, rode a saddle horse to town to meet the first train to arrive in Shaniko in 1900. His wife, Arlene Harris, was the daughter of Rosa and Jasper Harris. Their first son, Amos, was born in 1920 on his grandfather Fine's homestead. A second son of George and Arlene, Arthur, arrived in 1923. In 1926 when their daughter Georgene was born, the family was living in Portland.

During the Great Depression the Fine Family returned to Shaniko. Amos was eleven. The memories of Shaniko follow, cover the years 1931 to 1936.

"I could be known as the Shaniko Fiddler. I played for my first dance with my dad and others at Mandy Fine's house in the early '30's when people came from miles around for

Arlene Harris married George, the eldest son of John Fine. Their eldest son, Amos, became a fiddler like his father. Here Arthur and his father, George Fine, Georgene, Arlene, and Amos are shown in family group.

a night of dancing, eating, and visiting. I don't think there was $20 available in the entire crowd, but a collection was taken. I didn't get paid; didn't play much. The fiddle Dad bought in 1917 to play at dances in the Shaniko country was later given to me and I've been playing on it ever since.

"When Sue Morelli was running the Shaniko Hotel I went back to play for 'Shaniko Days.' I realized then that the fiddle had been used at Shaniko and Antelope over a period of 50 years. Playing fiddle has been my hobby. I had a little band 21 years."

In 1936 the Fine family moved to The Dalles where Amos began work for Pacific Power & Light Company. He was transferred to Madras forty miles from Shaniko, and again he played for dances in the area. He married Bonnie Butler in 1946. They have two boys and four girls.

Arthur, son of Frank Fine, retired after 20 years in the Armed Forces in 1959, then joined Lockheed Aircraft in California. Georgene, the only girl in Frank Fine's family, is department store manager at A.M. Williams Company in The Dalles. Her children, Glenda, Donna, Marie, Carolyn, David, and Mike Webber, live with her and her husband Al Jones.

Ebenezzer Fine, son of John E. Fine, left the Shaniko country before 1930, as did Alonzo and Frank. But before that, "Eb" Fine married Amanda "Mandy" Wilson. Eb ran the horse-drawn dray carrying produce to the store, delivered coal and wood to the townspeople from the warehouse, and did any other draying work he could. Their children were Myron, Harold, Allen "Dude," Jesse, and Welsey. Myron died while in his teens. Harold ran the Shaniko dray when his father moved to California. His wife, Thelma Ashley, was raised in southern Wasco County. Their children are Margaret (Welch), Charles "Buzz," Lewis, Darlene (Pollack) and Betty (Chamness).

Allen, brother of Harold, lived around Shaniko, working on farms and in the warehouse. He was a large, strong man. During World War I Allen served in the army, then was married and had one daughter. He died in the 1950's while living at Terrebonne.

Jesse R. "Touch" moved to California, and Wesley lives in Madras.

## James W. Fisher

Jim Fisher (1873-1958) was born in Salem, son of James Fisher and Mary Starkey, who pioneered in Oregon in 1852. When the six-year-old Jim went to live with his aunt, Mrs. Robinson in The Dalles (1893) there was no railroad up the Columbia River from Portland to The Dalles. The principal transportation was furnished by steamboat.

In 1900 Fisher went to Shaniko and worked in the warehouse until 1903. Then, in partnership with Jack Coe, he

When he first came to Shaniko, James Fisher was partner to J.H. Coe, operating a sheep ranch south of Shaniko. Eventually he owned the ranch and enlarged his acreage until he owned 25,000 acres.

bought 320 acres of land from Jones & Kelsay, and thus began a 40-year career in ranching and sheep raising. At one time he and Mike Reeder were in partnership. Jim gradually bought out land and homesteads until he owned 25,000 arces (30 sections of land) nine miles in length and two to five miles across. The place south of Shaniko is all fenced and is one of the best-watered ranches in Eastern Oregon.

Weigand Bros. bought the Fisher holdings in 1944, planning to raise cattle in place of the five bands of 1200 to 1500 sheep each that Fisher had kept. Fisher also raised hay and cattle, so his ranching operation was extensive. Of her father's labors, his daughter said, "The ranchers not only battled the weather, feeding and caring for the animals, but all the other things such as the hiring of men, setting up sheep camps, fencing property, running the main ranch, shearing sheep and selling wool—the two wars, the Depression, low prices. procuring food, the laws and restrictions of government leases in the national forest lands, and the

Left: In 1900 James Fisher went to Shaniko. Right: His wife Dolly and their daughter Helen.

transportation of sheep to that area—it is unbelieveable, I don't see how they did it.!"

In 1902 Fisher and Dolly Brown (1884-1962) were married. They had one daughter, Helen, born in 1913. The Fishers maintained a home in Shaniko, in addition to the one on the ranch, while Helen attended grade school. Then when she was ready for high school, they built a home on his property in The Dalles and Mrs. Fisher and Helen lived there with Jim alternating between the ranch and The Dalles.

Helen married Joe McMennamin. Their home is in Seattle.

## Claud Thomas Guyton

Claud Thomas Guyton was born June 8, 1889, at Grass Valley, Oregon. He was the youngest son of Willam F. Guyton, a Sherman County pioneer farmer and his wife, Ellen Smith. Claud homesteaded near Shaniko.

As a young man his talents fascinated the small children of his brother, Will Guyton, who remembered running to the

Jim Fisher's crew.

Wool buyers examining wool at Moody Warehouse.

Warehouse crew baling wool at Moody Warehouse.

Lambing time at the main ranch.

Handler and packer leaving for the summer range in the mountains. They were packed to follow sheep and set up camps in the forest. Ernest Starr was herder; Morgan Rothery was one of the men shown.

Ernest Starr, herder; packer not known. The picture was taken at Mt. Bachelor.

Jim Fisher's sheep in the Deschutes Forest near Mt. Bachelor grazing the meadow beside Spark's Lake.

Irma, Irene Hoech, and their cousin Mildred Smith, Helen Fisher.

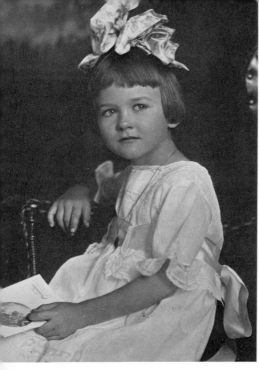

Jim and Dolly Fisher had one daughter, Helen, who played with the Hoech girls (when hairbows were the thing to wear).

All dressed up for a school play. From left: Irene Hoech, her cousin Mildred Smith, Irma Hoech, and Helen Fisher.

Children's party, back row: Helen Fisher, Mildred Smith, Irene Hoech, Jim Rees, Irma Hoech, Elton Bogart, Bob Hinton, Clifford Bogart, (?). Front row: Donald West, arm on shoulder of Jack Rees, John Reeder, Fred Fisk, Raymond Olsen, Jesse Fine.

door when they heard their Uncle Claud stride up on the porch, spurs klinking—a real cowboy, wearing long-haired, silky black chaps and a cowboy hat.

After dinner he would tilt his chair against the wainscoting and whittle wooden tops from their mother's empty spools. The children watched this with interest, but when, without changing position, he flipped a spool-top out to land on the floor spinning, they squealed with delight.

They had never seen a white cigarette. Cowboys rolled their own. Their father had been a cowboy, too, and smoked Bull Durham out of a little sack he carried, along with brown papers in his breast pocket. When Claud's right hand dipped in his left breast pocket and came out with the little white Bull Durham sack and tan paper, they watched intently. Sure enough, he could add tobacco to the paper he was holding in his lips, roll it with his right hand, lick the

137

Claud Guyton was a cowboy who could roll and light a cigarette with one hand. Bessie Whealy was the local school teacher. Claud had other accomplishments besides rolling cigarettes, for he courted and won Bessie's hand in marriage. Their wedding picture.

edges, run a thumb across to seal it, put it in his mouth, get a match from his pocket, strike it with his thumb nail, or on the seat of his pants, and light up without taking his left hand from his pants pocket.

Undoubtedly Claud Guyton had other accomplishments about which his nieces and nephew knew nothing. At any rate, he persuaded the new school teacher at Wilcox to leave her profession in June of 1917 to become his wife.

Bessie Madge Whealy was born August 15, 1892, in Redwood Falls, Minnesota, the eldest of seven children. She attended "teachers' college" at Monmouth, Oregon, then taught school at Grass Valley, Kent, and finally Wilcox, the country school where she met Claud Guyton. For her teaching labors, she received $55 a month, plus $2.50 for janitorial work. She lived with one or another family in the district, paying $3 a week for board and room.

138

Shortly after Bessie and Claud's wedding they asked Will Guyton's youngest child, Helen, age seven years, to visit them a week on Claud's homestead where they were living. There were few conveniences and the bride was lonely and homesick. She seldom saw another woman, the coyotes howled at night, and the only reading matter she had was magazines a year old loaned by a neighbor. Water was carried from a spring up the canyon and kept in a pail with a family dipper floating in it. When Claud "proved up" on the homestead they moved to the Fisher ranch. Claud worked there off and on for many years.

About 1933 he went to work for William Mitchell during the construction of the Wapinitia Highway. He also did farm work for Ben Taylor and for Muddy Company during 1944 and 1945.

Donald Dean Guyton was born May 26, 1918, and Gayle Garnet, March 22, 1921. The Guytons made their home in Shaniko during the school years of their children.

Dean entered the Service in March 1942, training at Shepherd Field, Texas, to be an airplane mechanic. As a member of the 45th Bomber Squadron he served in India, China, and Tinian in the Marianas. The group received a Presidential Citation. In November, 1945, he returned home. He and Helen Lee were married, May 29, 1948, and they made their home in Fossil. Helen taught school there 14 years. Dean was employed at Pine Corporation at Kinzua and later at Warm Springs Forest Products Industry.

Gayle married Dick Hahn, son of Leo Hahn of Muddy Company Ranch. They made their home at "Muddy." Later Dick sold the ranch and they ran cattle and lived near Woodland, Washington. The Hahns had two daughters, Carole, born November 12, 1943, and Linda, born October 16, 1949. Linda married Richard Parrett, who came from Alberta, Canada. They have daughters Kimberly Dawn, born October 15, 1972. and Leigh Nicole, who arrived February 9, 1977. The Parretts live at Molalla, Oregon.

Glade Guyton married an Antelope boy, Wayne McCulloch. They operated the service station and restaurant after Millie Pullen sold out.

In 1946 the Claud Guytons bought a small ranch on Eight Mile above the Dallles. They farmed until 1958, then moved to Dufur, Oregon, where Claud worked part-time for the city. Bessie died January 17, 1969, followed February 19, 1969, by her husband Claud.

## Glade Guyton (McCulloch Carrigan Steinmetz)

Glade Guyton, born September 24, 1906, near Kent, attended Normal School at Monmouth and in 1925 was teaching school at Lower Antelope when she met and married Wayne McCulloch, a local resident. During a period when they were living in Southern Oregon, their daughter Mary Ada "Pat" was born.

In 1934 Bill Rees bought out Millie and Harvey Pullen's restaurant-service-station and dance hall across the street from his home and rented it to Wayne and Glade

In 1940 Glade and Wesley "Slim" Carrigan were married. Slim was a good Mechanic.

McCulloch who had moved back to Kent. There were two long buildings, side by side. One, the "Owl Roost," originally had been a rooming house. These rooms were formerly rented to single men. This inner structure had been remodeled for family living quarters built behind a small restaurant. A kitchen, store-room and bath had been added. The other building was a small warehouse that had been moved a few blocks by Arch Hanna for a dance hall.

For several years, Millie and Harvey Pullen had been serving meals, selling gasoline and holding Saturday night dances in the dance hall adjoining the restaurant.

The McCullochs moved into the building, July 5, 1934. Several years later Wayne left, but Glade remained in business there after the divorce, selling Shell gas for over 35 years. In 1942 she bought the buildings and continued to operate a restaurant until World War II which, with its food stamp allotments, made it almost impossible to secure adequate supplies. She closed the restaurant. Among the women employed to cook during the restaurant days were Mrs. Frank Barlow ("Jack"), Mrs. Bessie Guyton, Mrs. Lavada (Lyle) Whealy, and Mandy Fine.

Glade was soon called upon to teach the remainder of the school year. She had several grades with a total of ten or twelve pupils. Among those attending were four Wilson children, Margaret Fine, two Martin boys, Margaret Olsen, daughter of Ivan and Margaret Rees Olsen, and several other children in addition to her own daughter, Pat.

The 19th of September, 1940, Wesley "Slim" Carrigan and Glade were married. He was a good mechanic, so in addi-

141

Left: Glade remained in Shaniko and sold Shell products over 35 years. Right: After Slim died, Glade and Vergil Steinmetz were married. Vergil was employed by Blue Line Company that stored grain in the Shaniko Warehouses and elevator under the government's Commodity Credit Corp.

tion to pumping gas part-time at the Shell station to relieve Glade, he did garage work with Bill Schilling. During World War II Schilling rented the Reid garage near the hotel and did repair work on State Highway trucks.

Slim's heart began bothering him. In 1957 he died in the hospital at Prineville and was buried in the Guyton plot at the Odd Fellows Cemetery near Kent. By this time Glade was selling only road supplies and Shell gasoline.

The 5th of September, 1958, she and Vergil Steinmetz were married. They continued to operate the station as she had been doing, until their retirement in 1970. The dance hall, which had ceased to be used when the McCullochs moved in, had long since been sold to the Douthit boys who tore it down and used it for lumber at the ranch they were operating near Antelope.

Among regular customers at Glade's Shell Station were several families of Warm Springs Indians going to or coming from Celilo during the salmon runs. They ate, gassed up, and often required repairs on their cars. "Sometimes they needed to have credit extended," Glade said. "And never once in all the years did one Indian fail to pay his full bill as agreed."


## Pat McCulloch and Bill Hanks

Mary Ada McCulloch, daughter of Wayne and Glade McCulloch, who was born on St. Patrick's Day in 1930 in Medford, Oregon, was soon answering to the name of "Pat" and still does. When she was nine months old her parents returned to the Kent area. Pat went to grade school in Shaniko and began high school in Moro at the Sherman County High School. Two years later arrangements were made for Shaniko students to attend Wasco County High School at Maupin, so she graduated there in the spring of 1948.

In August of that year she and William D. Hanks, Jr., were married and bought the Moody house. Bill was employed by the State Highway Department. Their son, Steven Laurence, was born June 23, 1949; their daughter, Rena Glade, arrived the 23d of August, 1950.

Bill Hanks had come to Shaniko during the construction of the Rural Electrification power lines as pole-setting boss for Thompson & Thompson. In 1957 Bill leased a restaurant and Richfield gas station in the west end of town. Pat served full meals until 1961, then short orders and homemade doughnuts.

In 1955, Pat substituted for Mrs. Maud Garrett, the Shaniko Postmaster, and Mrs. Edith Hastings, Postmaster at Antelope. On Mrs. Garrett's retirement in 1956, Pat was appointed Postmaster of Shaniko.

After Ivan Olsen had the general merchandise store he bought from Gavin-Wheeler torn down, Hanks bought the vacant lots and moved the post office building a block west to the store site, remodeled it, and named it "Pat & Bill's," and they left the station they had occupied. Bill bought a wrecker and C.B. radio and began a towing service in con-

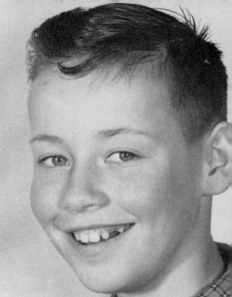

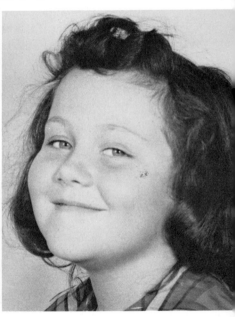

Top left: Bill Hanks came to Shaniko as pole-setting boss during the building of the REA lines. They bought the Moody place. Pat became the 10th postmaster at Shaniko. Top right: Their son, Steven, started school in Shaniko. Bottom left: After the Hanks family left Shaniko, Steven graduated from Reynolds High School. Bottom right: Rena Glade Hanks helped her mother prepare doughnuts to sell in the restaurant.

After graduating from high school, Rena attended Northwestern Business College in Portland.

Pat McCulloch and her cousin, Bill Rees, grew up together. Here they play in the sand on a hillside near the Guyton ranch about 1936.

Left: John McHargue was a carpenter who worked in and around Shaniko. His friend, John Keeney, is seated. Right: John McHargue proudly displays a bobcat shot at a forest camp in Idaho.

junction with the gas station and road supply shop. A small room was equipped to handle the mail and there Pat kept a post office, in addition to the work around the station. They bought a mobile home and installed it directly behind the station and sold the Moody house to Lloyd Harold.

The road over the high country is often slick. Some drivers, unaware of the dangerous conditions and lulled by long straight stretches, found themselves in the ditch. Once there was a spell of "blue snow" which fell over black ice. Road conditions were terrible. It was impossible to see the road, so there were many mishaps. Bill had 14 wrecker calls that day. Before the day was over, he became snow-blinded and Pat had to drive the truck for him. By this time Steven and Rena were high school students and both helped pump gas and take care of the road trade when their parents were away.

In the fall of 1966 the Hanks family moved their mobile home to the Troutdale area and the young people attended and graduated from Reynolds High School. Pat began work in the Portland Post Office. About that time Pat and Bill separated.

Steven is a barber-beautician in Portland. Rena married Myron Peterson. With their twins, Troy and Trina, the

Petersons live in Vancouver, Washington. Pat married Don Rose and their home is in Eagle Creek, Oregon.

Bill Hanks died in October, 1979. A memorial service was held October 15, outside the service station he had operated, overlooking the road to Antelope.

This spot had seen much of the history of Shaniko unfold. Here, along the sidewalk by the Pease & Mays Store there had been a sidewalk leading to the post office. This ground had been a tennis court and a place of fierce game rivalry betweeen the Shaniko youth. Ivan Olsen built an apartment in the store facing south, and it became the playground for their children. John and Mary Reeder lived in the apartment for years, so their daughter "Cookie" spent happy hours playing on the lawn.

The Hanks' mobile home was surrounded by this yard — a fitting place to hold a memorial service for Hanks who spent the happiest years of his life serving travelers passing through. The Rev. Larry Ferguson conducted the service; above his words was heard the barking of dogs, the passing of cars, and the roaring of trucks, but the sky was clear as the traffic pressed on to its destination.

## Robert "Bobby" Hinton

Robert "Bobby" Hinton, son of Richard and Minnie Wakerlig, was born in The Dalles, June 1910. The birth was a very difficult one and his mother Minnie was so dangerously ill that R.R. Hinton, fearing for his daughter-in-law's life, took her to Portland by ambulance. In time she recovered and returned to the Hinton ranch. She and Bobby's father "Dickie" were divorced.

Bobby was baptized by Bishop Paddock and named "Robert" after the Bishop.

Minnie and Bobby remained on the ranch several years;

Bobby Hinton remained at the Hinton
Ranch with his grandparents—a delight
to both the Hinton and Wakerlig families.

then Minnie went to Portland where she worked several years as a court reporter in the Multnomah County Court-house. Bobby remained at the ranch with his grandparents, a delight to both the Wakerlig and Hinton families. He started school at Bakeoven along with his cousins Pernita and Sonny Spalinger.

When word came to Minnie in Portland that Mary Lou was mentally ill and she should come and care for Bobby, she returned and took him with her to Shaniko. She got a job at the combined telephone and post office, working for Leola Loring.

Walter Lang, who had a homestead near the Ed Newcomb place, was working in Pease & Mays Store in Shaniko. He and Minnie married and lived on the W.F. Johnson homestead. Bobby attended the Shaniko school until he finished his freshman year, when the family moved to The Dalles where he completed high school.

Bob Hinton was an honor student at Eastern Oregon

College of Education at La Grande, a member of the second class to register at the school, in 1930. For a year and a half he attended college, working in a restaurant to make his way. When the Depression hit La Grande, the "Green Parrot" where he had worked was closed and he had to quit school. He remained in La Grande, not attending classes, and worked for a produce company and at the "Sacajewa Hotel" where he became a cook.

In 1935 he and Betty Mae Lilly were married, but they soon separated. After that, Bob cooked around in many restaurants in the United States from coast to coast. Eventually he settled in Portland and married Edna Ellen Fleming.

"Shaniko was quite a place," Bob Hinton said. "I was always proud I came from Shaniko."


## J.W. Hoech

J.W. Hoech was a medical doctor in Germany in the 1800's. His son Henry immigrated to the Kansas City area where he farmed and had a family. Around the turn of the century Henry Hoech took up a homestead near the present site of Grand Coulee Dam in Washington State, and settled his family, including his son J.W. Hoech, then a young man.

Young J.W. Hoech met and married Lulu Elder there. While both Hoech and Miss Elder were born near Kansas City, they first met at Heartline, Washington, where several of the Elder brothers, Lulu and her sister Minnie had taken homesteads. The younger brother Bob later took up a timber culture; the land sold for $3 an acre.

The Elder family were living in Kentucky when Lulu's father, John James-Elder, was born. He was seven years old when they left Kentucky. Mrs. Elder, also born in Kentucky, was named Featherstone. Besides the four girls, there were two brothers, James and Robert, in the Featherstone family.

After the marriage of J.W. Hoech and Lulu Elder, Hoech and a brother-in-law bought land in Central Oregon near Bend. The Hoech family and several members of the Elder family went to Bend to log off the timber. They found that developing the land would be too expensive, so after nearly a year there, they moved to Shaniko and Mr. Hoech worked in the store.

They couldn't find a house to live in, so moved in with the Fowlies. By this time they had a daughter, Irma, nearly a year old. Mr. Fowlie was in charge of the bank, having come from Arlington to manage the Eastern Oregon Banking Company. One of the employees, Jack Coe, left the bank to work with sheep so Fowlie hired Hoech. After Jack Fowlie's murder Mrs. Fowlie sold their home to the Hoechs. Their second daughter Irene was born there.

Describing her memory of the Fowlie case, Mrs. Hoech said, "Del Howell staggered drunk into the bank in the afternoon just before closing time, and shot Mr. Fowlie standing behind the teller's window. He might have shot my husband or Arch Altermatt. Dell banked there. We always thought he was asking for money or he had something against Mr. Fowlie that we didn't know. It was a terrible shock to everyone. A special train was prepared, and when it was ready they put Mr. Fowlie on it and sent him to The Dalles. He died before the train left town. Del was committed to prison for two years and served only about 18 months. He had a lovely family. His wife and a little girl were, of course, broken up. They moved to Salem and stayed there, which had a bearing on his getting out early. I never heard that the Howells ever came back to Shaniko."

The Hoechs moved to The Dalles the day The Dalles-California Highway was completed through Shaniko. The girls, Irma and Irene, attended school in The Dalles. Irma married Raymond Matthew; Irene became Mrs. Scott Milne.

A.R. Altermatt took over the bank and bought the Hoech house. After J.W. Hoech died his widow continued to

make The Dalles her home until her marriage to J.W.
Paullus of Spokane, Washington. She lived there until his
death, then returned to The Dalles.

## Andrew Holt

Andy Holt bought farm land near Kelsay Springs, up the
draw from the site where Fredrick Schilling set up the kiln to
make bricks for the Columbia Southern Hotel in 1900. He
farmed the land and built a good home on the property—
perhaps too expensive a place, because it was rumored that
it broke him. He soon sold out and farmed Bakeoven Ranch
for Clara Moody. He and his wife Phoebe Robertson Holt
were living in the ranch house at Bakeoven when it burned.

## James H. Keeney

James H. Keeney, operator of the Columbia Southern
Hotel, arrived in Shaniko in 1901. He was the son of Elias
Keeney, a Brownsville, Oregon pioneer of 1846, and his
second wife, Lucinda Van Winkle (sister of Homer Van
Winkle, one-time Atty. Gen. of Oregon.) Jim Keeney was
half-brother of Emma McHargue, whose husband operated
Hotel Shaniko. James Keeney remained in Shaniko until about
1906 (the last year he renewed his liquor license with the city
for the hotel).

Keeney remained a bachelor all his life. It has been said
that his finacee drowned in the Heppner flood. After leaving
Shaniko he returned to Brownsville.

## Richard I, Kinney, Long-time Postmaster

Dick Kinney was born on a farm in Sarcoxie, Missouri. He
was a veteran of the Spanish-American War who came to

Richard I. Kinney and Ethel McDonald were married at her home in Salem. Dick Kinney was postmaster of Shaniko almost 22 years, the longest time anyone served before or since. Ethel worked with him as well as tending the telephone office.

Oregon after his return to civilian life in 1898-9. He took up a homestead near Shaniko and lived there to prove up on it, walking to town several miles every day to work in Pease & Mays Store.

He and his wife Essie loved children and wanted to raise a family, but she had repeated miscarriages. Finally, in about 1916, she became so ill that she died before Dick could get the doctor out from Shaniko. Her dear friend Lillie Rees prepared her for burial; a costly service for Mrs. Rees as very soon thereafter she had blood poison in her hand. She spent several weeks in Portland trying to save her index finger. After surgery to remove the tendon, the hand healed but the remainder of her life that index finger on her right hand could not bend, causing burns and hurts because it stuck straight out.

In about 1917 Ethel McDonald arrived in Shaniko to work at the bank. In September 1918 she and Dick Kinney were married at her parents' home in Salem. This marriage did not produce any children, but both Dick and Ethel loved the children who came into the post office or were guests in their home. Where the Kinneys were, there were always toys to amuse the children who came in.

They raised a fine garden each summer. When asked how they achieved this when both worked, Ethel replied, "I worked in the garden at five o'clock while Dick got breakfast. After breakfast I'd go in the kitchen and he'd work in the garden until we went to work at 8 a.m."

Ethel McDonald, the youngest of five children, was born in Illinois in 1871. The family moved to Salem when she was 11 and though her health was frail, she finished school and attended business college. She worked for Barnes Cash Store, but soon had to get away from the dust and heat in the store.

Mr. Staley, who guided her through her business training, found her a job in the office of Eastern Oregon Banking Company in Shaniko. She arrived on the 5:20 p.m. train, along with about 20 other people and went to the hotel. It was her first night away from home. "I was a lonely little kid," she said, "and went to bed as soon as I reached my room. Arch Altermatt was expecting me and came to welcome me—and I had gone to bed! The next day the Hoechs invited me to dinner, and I soon got acquainted with the lovely people in Shaniko. Mr. Hoech and Arch Altermatt were running the bank. Business came from as far away as Ashwood, Horseheaven, and Madras.

"Altermatts moved to their homestead and I lived in their house that summer. When winter came I asked them to come back so they wouldn't have to drive the three miles in the cold to work. They slept on the couch in the living room with Darrel who was small. Bob was born later.

"Then I rented the house across the street. About that time the Cole Smith family came to Shaniko and there was no place for them to live, so they took the house I had rented and they boarded me.

"In March I took up a relinquished claim of Tom Blossick. Then in June I went home and stayed until September when Dick and I were married. Dick was sure full of fun! He was always so nice to me.

"After we were married, the Bogarts who were running the

post and telephone office, asked us to take it over so they could prove up on their land, and we did. When they left for Winnemucca, Nevada, we bought their house in Shaniko and lived there unitl we retired and moved to Madras."

Mrs. Kinney worked in the telephone office in Madras three years to complete proper time for her retirement; then they moved to a rural home near Salem, where Dick died about 1960. Mrs. Kinney moved into Salem to be near her sisters. They died one by one, and in 1975 she moved to the Methodist Home in downtown Salem. She died in July, 1981.

## The Kramer Family

Joseph "Joe" Kramer, born in Oshkosh, Wisconsin, in 1872, moved with his family from Minnesota to Vancouver, Washington, in 1913, then to Oregon in 1916.

His wife was Anna Weiss, born in Pierz, Minnesota, in 1874. There were seven children, all born in Minnesota: Joe, William "Bill," Charles, Veronica, Ernest "Ernie," Sylvester "Vesty," and Harold.

The year 1916 found Joe Kramer filing on a homestead in the Criterion area, in a place known as Fir Tree Canyon, on the breaks of the Deschutes River. In 1920 he moved to a wheat ranch on Ridgeway. It was then that Shaniko became his hometown. His son, Ernie, worked with his father on the farm for 7 or 8 years. When Ernie got married, Joe returned to the homestead, so was no longer around Shaniko.

Joe had two brothers, Henry and Ed. They came to Southern Wasco County about the time he did. They sold their homesteads to Joe, who farmed until ready to retire. He moved to Maupin in 1942.

The Kramers were the first to help any of their neighbors in time of need. During the flu epidemic in 1918 they worked practically all day and night for weeks helping people who were sick. They did not ever have the flu themselves.

Children of Joseph Kramer and Anna Weiss:

Joe stayed in North Dakota until 1921, then moved to Maupin.

William "Bill" spent much of his life in the Shaniko vicinity, working off and on at the warehouse, on road projects, for the city, and for Morrison and Knudsen. He spent his later years in Maupin working as custodian for the school. Bill married Ruth Ellwell. They had two children, Allan and Maxine Ruth. When the children were in high school, Bill and Ruth separated. Allan worked around Shaniko for a while. He eventually moved to Sparks, Nevada.

Maxine Ruth went to Shaniko grade school. When she was sixteen she married a boy by the name of Kaseberg from Wasco, but in a few weeks she was home with her father, Bill, and brother, "Buddy" (Allan). One morning the men folk got up to go to work at seven o'clock. It had been a cold night and they left a good fire burning, but Maxine didn't get up until ten when the fire appeared to be out. She got some gasoline and tossed it on the hot coals. It exploded, sending out flames which burned her and caught her night clothing on fire. She jumped back in bed to smother out the flames. When she saw the whole place was on fire, she rushed to Adelbert Rees's house next door with her charred clothing dropping away behind her. The burns were treated there. Her father was called and took her to The Dalles to the hospital. Three days later she died of the burns. Bill married again; both are deceased.

## Brothers and Sisters of Bill Kramer

Charles worked on heavy construction projects which kept him moving all over the United States. He died in Texas.

Veronica married Fred Curtis of Hood River. They lived in Hood River, then moved to Portland, Salt Lake City, Utah, and finally to Los Angeles.

Ernest "Ernie" married Aliene Green of Maupin. For 18 years he operated the E.K. Food Center there. He particualrly enjoyed fishing and hunting, but after retiring he took up woodworking and made handy novelty objects.

Sylvester "Vesty" married Florence Cavin. He owned and operated the General Mercantile Store in Dufur many years.

Harold went to West Covina, California, where he is employed in a manufacturing plant in the City of Industry, California, building electrical motors. He was in the Air Force Secret Service during World War II.

## Marion Lord

Marion Lord, Wasco County Health Nurse and veteran of World War I, worked in the early tuberculosis prevention project in Southern Wasco County and the well-baby clinics in Shaniko and Antelope during 1940-42. She made regular visits to the two towns, clearing up a source of TB infection in the Antelope area and encouraging better infant care.

Marion was born in Waupaca, Wisconsin, September 25, 1884, and finished high school there, then took nurses' training. She told of the gruelling life of nurses in the terrible days of World War I when the women would frequently begin their days in the early morning and not have a chance to eat again until nightfall. She said, "I used to hate rolled oats, but when I saw the girls fainting with fatigue before the day was over and realized that a good breakfast would have prevented it, I saw the value of eating good old rolled oats every morning."

She lived in The Dalles during her years as Wasco County Health Nurse. She was later to become school nurse at

Ellensburg, Washington, where she lived the remainder of her life. The American Legion, of which she was a member, conducted graveside services at her burial. Helen Rees received her watch, flag, and personal articles, which were presented to Marion Lord's godchild Richard Rees.

## James J. McHargue
### February 5, 1851-November 14, 1932

## Owner And Operator Of Hotel Shaniko

James J. McHargue was born in Brownsville, Oregon. His parents James K. and Sarah Jane Montgomery McHargue, were among the first party of immigrants to reach Brownsville, along with the Browns and Keeneys, On March 25, 1874, McHargue married Mary Emma Keeney (October 9, 1857-August 17, 1927), daughter of Elias Keeney. Elias and his brother Jonathan were "Mountain Men," serving with the hastily recruited soldiers sent to the scene of the Whitman Massacre, Elias Keeney was with the first members of the party to reach the site of the Whitman Mission after the tragedy, and he and his brother Jonathan helped bury the dead.

James and Emma McHargue moved from Brownsville to Waitsburg, Washington, then to Albany, Oregon, before going to operate Hotel Shaniko. After the hotel burned, the McHargues moved to Portland. He began the Mt. Scott Express business. His dray was pulled by two roan geldings that weighed 2,000 pounds each. After his wife's death he lived with his daughter in Shaniko, but died in The Dalles.

Children of the McHargues who grew to maturity were Lillie May, John Nathaniel (March 21, 1881-196?)—John was a carpenter who worked at various times in and around Shaniko—and Margaret Jane (January 13, 1881-January 7,

1967.) Her first husband was Angus Shaw of Mill City, Oregon, who died within a few years. She married Dr. Walter W. Hart, many years a practicing dentist in The Dalles. After Dr. Hart's death she returned to Brownsville where she and her younger sister Flo had a small home built. Flora Odessa "Flo" (November 12, 1888-1972) married Dick Armstrong who was foreman on construction of the Ariel Dam in Washington. He worked on various British Columbia projects. They raised two sons, James "Jim" and Angus "Gus."

## Al McKinley
### Husband of Mary Wakerlig

Little is known of the early life of Al McKinley. Those who knew him well remember that he talked much but said little about his childhood or parents. As a young man he herded sheep.

After his divorce from Mary Wakerlig, he, with help from his boys, had a race track out on "the Flat" to train horses for trick riding acts at local rodeos. His sons performed in these displays.

It was said Al was a "horsetrader" by nature who went to great effort to make a dollar from every transaction with stock. He bought up "bummer" lambs for a small amount and raised them by hand. Eventually, he had a little band of sheep which he pastured around town wherever the grass grew high. This reaped two good results: the sheep had free grazing and it eliminated the danger of fire around town when the grasses dried up in the summer.

If there was a card game at the Pastime, Al was there. He played with zest until his luck began to run out, then his sight got so poor he couldn't see the spots on the cards and had to cash in on his chips. In his later years Al watched Glade's Shell Service Station when she had to be out of town. "He was a good friend to me," she said. Al died, date unknown.

## Nelia McLellan (Kentner Bergstrom)

Nelia McLellan was born July 24, 1896, in Persia, Tennessee. Her father, Joseph Theodore McLellan, went to Shaniko in 1902 to work for Henry C. Rooper. On November 28, 1904, his wife and their three daughters, Nelia, Mamie, and Nina Lee, arrived from Tennessee after traveling six days and seven nights on the train. Joe McLellan homesteaded one mile west of the present highway out on Ridgeway southwest of Shaniko. The family moved to the homestead in 1907, after he left the Rooper ranch. Mrs. McLellan took a "desert claim" at "Big Cove" on the Deschutes River.

Archibald Kentner of Kent and Nelia McLellan were married February 1, 1915. Their children were Mabel Frances, June 26, 1916; Ida Lee, November 4, 1917; Theodore Wilbur, January 22, 1920; Miles Arch, September 4, 1921. The family lived in the Kent vicinity. The couple separated in May 1926 and Nelia went to Bend. On May 12, 1934, she married William Lewis Bergstrom from Iowa, who had lost his wife and children in a fire. The family lived in Bend.

## John McLennan

John McLennan and two other Scotsmen immigrated to Montana expecting to make money running sheep. They were soon joined by John's younger brother Duncan. John

left Montana and on April 15, 1898, was married to Dolly
Warrak in The Dalles. They had one daughter, Mary
Elizabeth Marguerite, who was baptized Roman Catholic
in 1908.

John appeared in Antelope as a bachelor sheepman. He
made money with his herds and in 1921 bought the Shaniko
Hotel. For about 25 years numerous people managed the
hotel until Johnny retired and made it his home. After
Johnny was abducted his health was broken and he was no
longer able to manage the hotel, but was taken to The
Dalles where he died around 1940.


## Duncan McLennan

Duncan McLennan went to Shaniko when his brother John
disappeared and remained to operate the Shaniko Hotel. He
often visited at Glade's station, sometimes talking about
his childhood in Scotland. When he was a little boy he went
with his mother to church—barefoot—to save his shoes.
When they arrived she would wipe off his feet and put on his
shoes before they entered the church.

When Duncan came to the United States to join his
brother, he left his wife and three children in Scotland,
expecting to send for them soon. Before he could do that
his wife suddenly died. The children remained in Scotland.
He never remarried.

Duncan had a fine Scotch burr and a great joy in living.
After his brother John died, Duncan, a generous man,
brought the old sheepherders and stockmen who had small
ranches out on the "breaks" of the canyons to the hotel,
when they were too old or sick to remain on their little
holdings. Duncan took care of them until they died. Among
the men who lived at the hotel were "Big" McKay, Gus
Bowen, Walter "Waddy" McPherson, "Little" Johnny Joyce,
and Warner Spalinger. Frank Wagner ate meals there during

Lillie Rees congratulates Duncan McLennan on his 80th birthday.

the war. There was little road traffic, so the hotel was essentially closed to the public. Duncan kept busy raising a "Victory Garden" north of the hotel, raising many of the vegetables consumed there.

When Duncan was past 80 years old he went to Glade's in his "Kilties" and brought his bagpipes. He laid newspapers to make a cross on the center of the floor, then did the sword dance. "Well, yes, he took a little of the liquid inspiration— to relax him—you know," said Glade.

Friends and relatives gathered from as far away as Montana to help Duncan celebrate his 90th birthday. Sue Morelli helped make it a festive occasion. Jimmy Rees brought a friend from Portland to play the bagpipes. Duncan enjoyed every bit of the party.

When the Episcopal minister from the Dalles came, Duncan would walk to the schoolhouse for the Evening

Prayer service with Glade and her family. He often fell asleep in church, perhaps because he had lost most of his hearing and it was hard to remain awake when he couldn't hear.

Duncan's years stretched from September 20, 1873, to December 5, 1966. He was buried at the Odd Fellows Cemetery in The Dalles. Pallbearers reflected the Irish friends as well as Scotsmen who appreciated the life of Duncan McLennan: Pat McHugh, James Cameron, Neil McDonald, Don McIntosh, Roddy McAuley, John Silvertooth, Murdo McIntosh, John Joyce, Ed Cunnion, Frank Harris, Sam McKay and Donald Maurer. The Rev. Ernest Tayler officiated.

## Willliam Hovey Moody
## 1860-1919

William Hovey Moody ("Will" or "Bill") was born on October 5, 1860. His father, Zenas Moody, was Oregon's seventh governor.

When, in 1901, Bill Moody was sent to manage the Moody Warehouse in Shaniko, his children were in high school. His wife, Clara McFarland Moody, maintained their home in The Dalles during the school year, then joined her husband with the children for summer vacation. In a few years Bill bought the Shaniko Warehouses from Moody Company of The Dalles and enlarged the original building, then built smaller warehouses for specific usage, such as for barley, hay, coal, coal-oil and gasoline. Still later, Moody bought out the large wool warehouse built by the Townsite Company, called the Shaniko Warehouse, and operated all the warehouses in Shaniko and made money doing so.

Bill Moody was a brusque speaker but a good businessman. He was known to say what he thought. The following letters reveal a glimpse of the characters of two strong men who did much to shape the business life of the growing town. Mr. W. Lord was in charge of rentals for Townsite Company. The second cottage mentioned adjoined the lot on which the Moodys were living.

The cottages were eventually purchased by Moody, presumably for his price.

Fifteen years before his death, Bill Moody was confined to a wheelchair as a result of a stroke.

Portland
Aug. 21st 1910

Mr. W.H. Moody
Shaniko Ore.

My Dear Sir:-

Just received a letter from Coe, that you offered $700 for the two houses I owne, which I cannot take as they are worth more, no matter if Shanoko don't grow. Shaniko always will be a good place and the emigration is going to take up all the land that can be farmed. The lowest cent I would take is $1000. and should you wish them at that price all right.

The wheat outlook is bad for prices and it is thought by wheat buyers that it will go lower, as the export trade cant pay the present prices.

Very truely yours,
W. Lord.

Sept. 12, 1910.

Mr. W. Lord,
Portland, Oregon.
Dear Sir:

Replying yours of the 21st ult., will say that I am

still willing to pay you $700.00 for your two cottages and am not very particular whether I get them at that figure or not.

They are both getting rather rickety and if you decide to hold them I shall expect you to overhaul the one I am living in and make it habitable for the coming winter.

The other cottage is also settling and will need new underpinning before winter sets in.

Very truly yours,
W.H. Moody

## Clara McFarland Moody
## 1861-1933

Clara McFarland was born in The Dalles to James Cornelius McFarland (1833-1893) and Martha Anne Bouton (1834-1907.) McFarland was engineer on the steamboat *Wasco*, plying from The Dalles to the Cascades on the Columbia River. This is the steamboat that resuced the whites at Stevenson, Washington, during the massacre of 1856. James McFarland had crossed the plains in 1852 and settled at The Dalles.

Music was an important part of Clara Moody's life. She often sat at the piano after dinner playing for her guests. First they heard a melody, then they gathered around the piano singing any tune requested; Clara could play an unfamiliar song if someone hummed it. The Moody's son Adelbert was musical as well, and often they and Bill Rees would sing and record their songs on the old Edison cylinder phongraph.

One of the sad events in the life of the Moody's was the loss of their little daughter Mamie (Mary) who fell into a container of scalding water. She died of the burns.

Right: The children of Bill and Clara Moody; Mary, Adelbert and Druscilla. Left: Clara Moody loved pretty clothes. Her granddaughter, Elyse West, once said she loved to give her grandmother a pretty handkerchief because she knew how much fun she'd have buying a new outfit to match it.

Clara loved pretty clothes, and since she came from a well-to-do family and married into one, she could buy about whatever she chose. Her grandaughter, Elyse West, once said, "I just love to give Grandmother a pretty handkerchief for her birthday because I know how much fun she can have choosing a costume to match it." Perhaps this was an exaggeration, but Clara bought and wore expensive clothes and furnished their home with taste. It was the Moodys who set the social scene in the early years at Shaniko.

Children of Bill and Clara Moody were Adelbert (1883-1954), Drusilla (1887-1951) and Mary (1885-1893).

Adelbert attended Bishop Scott Academy in Portland and Rush Medical School in Chicago. He became a well-known pathologist in the San Francisco area. With his wife Mabel and daughter Blanche, he lived in San Francisco.

Drusilla married Howard Melville West. (He died in 1919.) Their children were William Melville (1911-about 1972) who was a Merchant Marine, Elyse (1914) and Donald (1915). Elyse married H. Lee Clark in 1936; their home is in Portland. Donald is in the insurance business. He has worked in San Francisco and Los Angeles.

## Zenas Ferry Moody
### May 27, 1832-1917

Zenas Moody established the second warehouse business in
Shaniko. He was born in Granby, Massachusetts. He sailed
from New York for Oregon via Panama in 1851. Moody
became a surveyor and worked in Oregon in 1856, in California with General Freeman's party, and finally in Illinois.
When in 1861 men were enlisting as volunteers for the protection of Washington, D.C., there was Zenas Moody in
uniform.

The West called him again and by 1862 he had a mercantile store in The Dalles and one in Brownsville, another pioneer community. It was in Brownsville that he
met and married a perky young lady who defied her
guardian and came to Oregon with a wagon train,
working her way cooking and herding cattle for friends
as they came to Oregon in 1852.

The Moodys made their home in The Dalles. It was
from that city that the Moody activities exploded in all
directions:

1865-67    He operated a transportation company in Eastern
           Oregon, Idaho and Washington. He built a boat
           *Mary Moody* on lake Pend O'reille in Northern
           Idaho, and organized the Montana-Oregon-Idaho
           Transportation Company to get supplies to the
           mines in Montana.

1867-69    He was operating a mercantile business in Boise,
           Idaho and extending his activities around The
           Dalles to become Wells Fargo Company's agent
           and mail contractor between The Dalles and
           Portland.

1872       Moody became State Senator from Wasco County,
           receiving both Democratic and Republican
           nominations.

1874      The mail contract between The Dalles and Portland was awarded Moody, so he established a steamer run above and below the Cascade Rapids. This run required that mail be portaged between the two steamers as it was not possible to negotiate the rough water. That winter the Columbia River froze over, making it necessary to carry the mail by pack train from the Cascade Rapids to The Dalles. The next spring he sold his boats to Oregon Steam & Navigation Company.

1880      He was chosen Speaker of the Oregon House of Representatives.

1882-87   He served as Governor of Oregon. His term in office was the longest single term in Oregon history, because the Legislative Assembly changed its meeting time from June to September. He held office four years and four months.

The square block now occupied by the State Library is the site of the home Moody built in Salem. He was thought of as a good governor and could probably have been elected to a second term, but he chose not to run; instead, he returned to The Dalles and his mercantile business, bank, and the warehouse there.

In 1900 the plans for the City of Shaniko attracted his attention as a place to expand the warehouse business. By 1902 the Moody Warehouse Company was in town ready to do business in the large storage building just completed. Managing the new branch was the son of Zenas Moody, William Hovey Moody.

Zenas and Mary Moody spent their later years quietly in Salem.

The Moodys had five children:

Malcom Adelbert (born Nov. 30, 1854)—congressman, warehouseman, mayor of The Dalles. He was also a rancher.

He worked to improve The Dalles — Celilo Canal.

Zenith Arizona (born April 7, 1857)—a mechanical engineer.

William Hovey (born October 5, 1860)—who managed, then owned the Shaniko branch of Moody Warehouse.

Ralph Elmo (born August 27, 1867)—who was for years attorney for the SP&S Railroad Company, then attorney general of Oregon. He was president of Old Wasco County Pioneers Association in 1939.

Edna (born July 8, 1869) — whose husband was Eugene P. McCornack.

## Mary Stephenson Moody
### Wife of Governor Zenas F. Moody

Mary Stephenson was orphaned at eight and lived four years with the Thomas Henry family in Illinois. When she was 16 the Henrys decided to move to Oregon. When her guardian refused to give her permission to go with them, she went to Madison to see them off. Before they left in March, 1852, she asked if she could go with them and work her way. It was agreed she could go it she'd do the cooking and drive the cattle. She knew that before word could reach her guardian, she would be on her way. He learned about her going when her letter reached him from Oregon six months later.

Mr. Henry was an old man and she was needed to ride after his large herd—all of which died from exhaustion before they reached Oregon.

There were about twenty-five young girls, probably fifty young men, and many married couples. so the evenings were jolly times for singing and talking. There were some ministers and a few college graduates who conducted daily Bible Study classes, and there were many lectures.

It was late in June when they reached the Platte. The stream was a bad one, so they took the emigrant's dugout ferry, formed of six dugout canoes lashed together with slabs. The charge was $5.50 for each wagon, 50¢ an animal and $1 each person.

On July 22 they came to Fort Hall. The houses were adobe and they saw scores of Shoshone Indians around the fort. At Steamboat Springs the cattle were very thirty, and as soon as they smelled the water they ran to it. When they put their noses in the boiling water they bawled, whirled around and stampeded. It was a pretty thrilling sight to see 25 wagons stampeding over the plains.

At Shoshone Falls they saw Indians spearing salmon and bought some. They found the falls impressively beautiful.

Mr. Henry had started with 15 yoke of cattle and 35 head of loose cows and horses. Only three yoke survived the trip. The last of the loose animals was so weak he fell into the Columbia River at Shell Rock Point.

They struck the Umatilla River (called Utilla) September 3. When they reached The Dalles the whole beach of the Columbia River was covered with tents of the settlers waiting to go to the Willamette Valley, probably 1,000 people. If Mr. Henry could have brought all his cattle through, he would have been well-to-do, for in those days a man's wealth was measured by the number of his cattle.

The Henrys had every convenience in their two-story brick home, but when they reached the Willamette Valley they moved into a cabin without a fireplace and with only a rough, unfinished board floor. There was plenty of air as the logs were unchinked. The table was a slab run through the unchinked logs. Bedsteads were slabs crudely put together. The Henrys settled at Union Point, three miles from Brownsville.

## Joe and Sue Morelli

Joe and Sue Morelli met during his stay at Good Samaritan Hospital in Portland. Joe, a cowboy and rancher from the

Joe Morelli.

Sue Morelli.

Joe and Sue Morelli operated the Shaniko Hotel during the "Ghost Town" days and kept people who were wards of Wasco County. Meals were available family style in the dining room.

Morelli family: Mary Sue, Sue, Joe, Bonny Jo. The girls grew up in the Shaniko Hotel. Husbands of both girls drowned in separate accidents fording different rivers on horseback, about two years apart.

Shaniko area, was hospitalized from the dreaded Rocky Mountain spotted fever. Sue was his nurse. Upon his recovery, they married and lived for a while on a ranch outside of Shaniko. Because of an old injury sustained when Joe operated a riding academy in Portland, his back began giving him problems. Soon he was confined to a wheelchair. It was in 1954 that they bought the Shaniko Hotel from Duncan McLennan.

The Morellis had two daughters, Mary Sue, born July 13, 1949, and Bonny Jo, born July 29, 1951.

A number of retired local sheepmen, herders, and ranchers were living at the hotel when the Morellis bought it. Sue enlarged that number by bringing in county ward patients—elderly, but still able to get around with supervision. They had the freedom of the town, and Sue was a kind housemother as well as an efficient nurse in case of sickness—and Joe could stay in his beloved Shaniko.

"Many a day was made brighter," Sue said, "when Bill Rees sauntered in on his way to the post officed and, with

The county wards, Henry the "Cop" and Harold the sheriff, loved the make-believe of "Ghost Town" days, appearing around town with badges and toy guns for tourists to photograph. It was all a part of the western-days pretense.

his bottomless bag of witty sayings, would leave us all laughing." When he became ill, Sue was called to the Rees home and she accompanied him to the hospital in Prineville where she nursed him the last few days he lived. She said, "His passing ended an era in Shaniko. His end was like the fall of a mighty oak tree."

In June 1967 Bonny's husband, Lyle Johnson, was drowned in the Deschutes River near Maupin while attempting to ford the river on horseback. Two years later in June 1969, Mary's husband, Ike Palmer, was crossing the John Day River on horseback and was drowned. Both girls have remarried: Mary to Wayne Wolverton (they live in The Dalles); Bonny to Kevin Abendechein (Madras is their home).

## Millie Inman Holt Nicholson

Millie Inman (1854-1943) was born in the Midwest, married Lester Holt and had two children, Minnie (1874-

1955) and Lester. While the children were small, Millie decided to leave home and husband—against his will, if the story told by her son Les was correct. She packed up the children and headed her rig west. When her husband found she had gone he asked the State Police to stop his wife, daughter, and son at the state line. He underestimated Millie's ingenuity and determination. She had cut Minnie's hair and dressed her in boy's clothing—thus eluding the planned detention.

She and the children lived in the Willamette Valley, Prineville, and finally in Shaniko. Times were very hard and she took in washing, worked out, and scrimped to make ends meet.

The Rees family remembers Grandma Nicholson coming to cook and tend house while Lillie Rees was in Portland doctoring a badly infected hand. Millie kept the family fortified with good Irish stew made with plenty of well-fattened mutton—nourishing, but not the family's accustomed fare. She was a goodhearted soul to whom life had been less than kind, but the harshness of her life did not impair her physical stamina, for she lived to be 89 years old, doing for herself and living in her own home in Shaniko.

Millie's daughter Minnie married Louis Bleakney (1865-1923). He was the son of early residents of the Bakeoven area, John Bleakney (1823-1913) and his wife Mattie Bellows. Louis Bleakney had a brother Tenny. Shortly after the marriage of Lou and Minnie they moved to Sourdough Flat below Bakeoven. Two boys and a girl were born to them: Theodore "Teddy" born at Scott's Mills, Oregon, in 1892; Le Roy G. "Lg" born December 18, 1893, and Ethel (Schadewitz) December 18, 189?.

Minnie lived in Shaniko or kept a residence there most of her life, although she often worked elsewhere. Her son Lg married Alice Leora Brown, September 14, 1914, in Goldendale, Washington. She was the daughter of Anna May Fine and Walter Bullard Brown. Lg and Alice were parents of a

In his later years, Les Holt sat on the bench outside the hotel spinning yarns with anyone who would listen. He is shown here with the long-time marshal, Gus Reeder.

son, Darrel Alvin Bleakney (December 20, 1916-January 15, 1977) born in Grandma Nicholson's house in Shaniko.

Darrel Bleakney married Arlene Verena Ward, September 30, 194?, in Goldendale, Washington. Their daughter, Diane Bleakney Nash, lives in Milwaukie, Oregon.

To go back, Lg and Alice Brown were divorced and he married Elma Reeder. They had two daughters, Marjorie who lives in Michigan, and Evelyn, deceased.

## Les Holt Family

Grandma Nicholson's son Les and his wife Belle had six children: Frank, Millard, Madeline, Russell, and twins, Adrian and Alma. Frank and his sister, Madeline Carson, were raised by Grandma Nicholson. Madeline now lives with her brother Frank in the Beaverton area.

Adrian was a young grade-school student when the children were playing "Billy Goat" and enthusiastically butting heads like goats. This caused an injury to Adrian that resulted in his death. Lillie Rees laid him out for burial in the suit of one of her sons.

In his later years Les often sat on the bench outside the hotel in the summer, inside the lobby in winter, spinning yarns with anyone who would listen. H.L. Davis stayed in Shaniko while gathering material for his prize-winning novel, *Honey In the Horn*, and engaged Les in long conversations. Some of his Shaniko stories may have preserved Les's yarns, embellished, of course, with Davis's own writing style.

Les was a fiddler in some demand to play and call for square dances around the country. Another of his accomplishments was rooting for the home team at baseball games. Before public address systems were invented, Les's voice could easily be heard outfield. The team knew his favorite cheer by heart, "Mouth like an alligator, teeth like a saw, Antelope, Antelope, Haw, Haw, Haw!"

## Peder Johan Olsen

Peder "Pete" Olsen was born November 12, 1876, in Mo, Hemmes, Norway, about 35 miles south of the Artic Circle, on the River Rana. When his parents immigrated to the United States, Peder remained in Norway with his grandparents, Skipper and Mrs. Nils Nilson. The Nilson family owned the Selfers Locks extending from the fiord to the River Rana. Skipper Nilson built his own boats and exported fish from his fishing fleet. In 1889 Peder and his sister joined their parents and ten brothers and sisters near Silverton, Oregon.

Pete Olsen Family in 1949. Left to right: Pete, Mattie, Alice, Ivan, Raymond, Gertrude. Pete Olsen became Road Superintendent in Shaniko in 1917. The Olsens operated the Columbia Southern Hotel. Their son, Ivan, bought out Gavin-Wheeler Company store.

Peder soon became known as "Pete." He married Mattie Woodside in 1903. The Woodside family moved from Silverton to pioneer in the Wapinitia country in 1888. Mattie's grandfather was a survivor of an 1847 tragedy occurring at Box Elder Creek, Wyoming, when the Vaughn Company of wagons crossed the plains. Numerous emigrants in that company died of food poisoning which was believed to have been caused from eating fruit cooked and allowed to stand in a brass kettle. The senior Woodsides died and were buried in a common grave with the other victims. Children orphaned by this catastrophe were brought on to Oregon; among them was Mattie's grandfather. The people looking after the orphans died before the children were grown, so little is known of the Woodside family or where they came from.

Pete Olsen became Road Superintendent and moved to Shaniko in 1917. In 1927 he and Mattie operated the Columbia Southern Hotel. Pete became a member of the

City Council, but soon the family, except Ivan, moved to Klamath Falls. Mattie lived there many years until she went to Salem to live with Raymond and family.

Children of Pete and Mattie Olsen were Alice, Ivan, Raymond, and Gertrude.

Alice's married name was Vitus. Her husband died December 10, 1948. They had no children. Alice was the first "female" in the printing business in Oregon, in the 1950's. She continued in the business in Klamath Falls for 40 years, until her retirement in 1975.

Ivan, born in 1908, attended school in Shaniko. When 11 years old he began work as delivery boy after school and Saturdays at the Gavin-Wheeler store. After graduating he clerked in the store, then managed it for Mr. Gavin. On September 17, 1928, Olsen married Lillian Margaret Rees, daughter of Mr. & Mrs. W.A. Rees. Margaret died in May 1930, at childbirth, leaving Ivan with a daughter named Lillian Margaret, after her mother. Margaret grew up in the Rees home and graduated in 1947 from Maupin High School.

In 1936 Tom Gavin died and Ivan Olsen bought the business. He married an Antelope teacher, Clola Gallegly, April 15, 1938. They partitioned off part of the hardware section of the store and lived in an apartment there. In 1943 Ivan bought the Cashman Store in Madras, hired John Reeder to manage the Shaniko Store, and moved his family to Madras. By 1960 Ivan had decided to close the store in Shaniko and had the building torn down. The lumber was used in the building of several houses in Madras.

The children of Ivan and Clola were Barbara and Carol Jean.

Barbara married Dudley Thomas of Madras and they and their children, Susan and Brian, live in Portland. Carol married Joseph Esquibel, who with a son and daughter live in Washington, D.C.

Pete's son Raymond worked 45 years for the Oregon State Highway Department. He had one son and two grandsons. Salem is his home.

The youngest of Mattie and Pete Olsen's children, Gertrude, was married to Gordon Shirley. Both were employed by the County Tax Department at Hanford, California. The Shirleys have two children and six grandchildren.

## Andrew (Andreas) Patjens Family

Deidrich Patjens and Elizabeth Bade of Germany were parents of Andrew Patjens, born December 5, 1879, at Ritchmoor, Hanover, Germany. In 1894 the gregarious Andrew immigrated to America with his parents and brothers, Deidrick and Heinrich, and sisters, Margaretha and Dorothea, and settled in the Bakeoven country. About 1908 Adele Sophie, daughter of Heinrich Meier and Charlotte Jade of Germany, came to the United States and went to work for Farghars nearby. The two young people met at Farghars and were married in Portland, January 10, 1912. When they returned to Shaniko on the train after the wedding, deep snow made it impossible for them to go on to Bakeoven so they spent several days honeymooning at the Columbia Southern Hotel.

Andrew was a talkative man but his bride was shy and while she learned to speak some English, she never learned to read it or write. She preferred German and they visited almost exclusively with German-speaking families; or she stayed at home except when they attended the Lutheran services in The Dalles. She was instrumental in having the two sons, Ernest and Andy H., stay with the Detjen family to be instructed and confirmed by Rev. Eck in The Dalles. She was somewhat interested in Christian Science writings and read them in a German edition. Andy owned some of the

Left: Ernest Patjens remained on the ranch where he raised feed hay, grains and stock. He now raises his own breed of cattle. Right Andy H. Patjens became grounds superinten-dent for the Christian Science Center at Bella Vista, Arkansas.

fertile wheat land near Bakeoven and through the years, added many homesteads to his holdings. He died, Nov. 26 1967, at age 88; his wife Adele died September 29, 1960, at 77 years.

Ernest, the older of the Patjens boys, born October 27, 1912, took after his father and the two got along well. After the Bakeoven School closed, the family lived during the school week in Mrs Nicholson's house in Shaniko, then during high school the boys boarded the school week with Reeders at Cross Hollows. After his return from the service in World War II, Ernest took over the ranch where he raised feed, hay and seed grains, and ran cattle. He married Ethel Douglas. They had no children. In later years he bought and sold stock. Now, retired, Ernest lives near The Dalles but keeps his hand in the stock business by raising his special breed of cattle.

Andy H., shy like his mother, was born September 21, 1913, on the Theis homestead. The farm operations were extensive and the men worked long hours. One of their chores was to haul water to the cistern with a four-horse team on a 500 gallon tank filled at one of two springs in the canyon. They hand-pumped water from the cistern for house use until George Witter of Kent was engaged to drill a well; then they installed a windmill and built a water tower so water was available by gravity flow—this, of course, besides the year-round farm work and care of the stock.

Andy told the story of a farm dog named Tip who oversaw ranching operations near the house. They sometimes kept horses in the yard with the gate closed so they couldn't get out. One evening they forgot to close the gate. The next morning there was Tip by the gate where he had spent the night keeping the horses from going out. "We seldom give our dogs enough credit for their intelligence," said Andy H.

After Ernest joined the service and Andy H. was through college, he felt he couldn't do the work of the two boys so he left to take a job in Portland. From there he moved to San Francisco and after his marriage to Janet Esther Wagner, they moved to Bella Vista, Arkansas, where he is grounds superintendent at the Christian Science Center. They have no children.

## Leslie Boice Payne

Leslie Payne was born June 6, 1872, in Boise Idaho. His wife, Martha Mabel Altermatt, was a sister of Mrs. John C. Fowlie and Archer Altermatt. Mabel Altermatt Payne was born in Springfield, Minnnesota, April 24, 1881. Leslie worked for the City of Shaniko as maintenance man from 1907 to about 1914. The family lived at Cross Hollows while Payne was water superintendent.

The children of the Payne family were Homer (died as a child), Culver Sist, John Kenneth, Ronald Nelson, Harold Altermatt, and Helen Doris.

They moved to the Fleck Orchard near Rufus about 1914.

The Leslie Payne Family lived at Cross Hollows while Payne was Water Superintendent—Kenneth, Culver, Ronald, Harold, Mrs. Payne, Lois, Mr. Payne.

## Children of Gustav H. and Wilhelmina Reeder

Elsie, the eldest of the Reeder children, was born August 25, 1901. She married John Thomas "Tommy" Jones, son of Al Jones, a pioneer to the Antelope country. Tommy was employed by Vernon Flatt Truck Line, hauling freight, express, and mail, from The Dalles to Antelope six days a week. Elsie spent many years working as clerk in the Shaniko, Antelope, and Moro post offices.

John Thomas Jones and Elsie Reeder had three children: Theresa, John Thomas II "Bud," and Doris. Theresa married George "Joe" Hood. They made Dufur their home. The Hood children are Michael "Mike" who moved to Florence; Janice, who works for the United States National Bank of Oregon at Newberg; and Ronald "Ronnie" now in Florence, who for a time was a clown in the rodeo circuit. John Thomas II, a farmer, lives with his wife Edna at Alicel, Oregon. Doris married Claud Bayer from Grass Valley. They live at Gladstone.

Left: Gus and Wilhelmina Reeder in 1950. Right: Elsie Reeder married Tommy Jones.

The G.H. Reeder Family from left: John, Gus, Wilhelmina, Elsie, Elma, Ralph.

Left: Elma Reeder married Lg Bleakney. Right: Ralph Reeder became a glider pilot.

Elma Reeder, born September 18, 1903, married Lg Bleakney. They operated the Owl Cafe several years in Albany Oregon. When they were divorced, her sister Marguerite Starr and her husband Clarence bought the restaurant. Elma married Virgil Lindsoe who died in recent years. Elma returned from South Dakota to live in Tigard, Oregon.

Ralph "Lanky" Reeder was born March 18, 1909 and attended school in Shaniko, though he did not finish high school. Before joining the Air Corps, he attended Adcox Automotive School in Portland. In the Air Corps he became a glider pilot, his years of service being 1940-45. In 1940 he married Georgia Warren. They settled in Portland where she worked for Ungar's until her retirement. Ralph worked at auto repairs, then as an electronic technican. Since his

Left: John and Mary Reeder with Cookie. John operated Ivan Olsen's Red & White Store, previously Pease & Mays. Right: Teresa Reeder grew up to teach school at Kent and had the sadness of being displaced at the end of an era when Kent School was discontinued, just as her father had been when the Shaniko store was torn down.

retirement he has worked part-time as a veterinarian's assistant.

John Douglas Reeder was born October 27, 1912, in Shaniko, as were all the Reeder children. John's first job was delivery boy at the Gavin-Wheeler Store when he was 11 years old. After finishing high school he clerked in the store until the Depression, when he was let go; then he worked for Dick Jordan building a water wheel at Two Springs above Maupin to irrigate Jim Hinton's property. He worked for the State Highway Department out of Shaniko and Maupin until 1941. That year he went to Alaska with Ed Bordwell, contractor, to put in a fueling system at Elmendorf Air Force Base out of Anchorage. He was on the job from November first to March first when he was injured by a large cement mixer and hospitalized for three months. When he returned from Alaska he worked at the Alcoa Aluminum plant in Vancouver, Washington.

On a visit to Shaniko, he learned Ivan Olsen's wife Clola was trying to operate the store alone while Ivan was getting settled in the Madras business. Ivan asked him to stay and operate the Shaniko store, and he did so.

184

In 1949 John married Mary Walkup (McDougall) who brought her daughter Sharon to live with them and attend school in Maupin. She finished eighth grade at St. Mary's Academy in The Dalles with her former class, went to school at Maupin to be queen of the Junior Prom, then attended nursing school in La Grande. She married Fred "Bud" Bower. They live in The Dalles where she has worked many years in The Dalles Hospital.

John and Mary's daughter, Teresa Rene "Cookie," was born December 22, 1952. As soon as Cookie was kindergarten age, John drove her to Grass Valley five days a week and Mary tended the store. The schoolboard decided that, "If they want so much for her to attend that they will drive 27 miles in all kinds of weather, we don't need to charge tuition." There was no school in Shaniko when she started first grade so she was taken to Mobleys, seven miles north, to ride the rest of the way to Kent on the bus with the Mobley children.

From 1943 to 1960 John ran the store and lived in the apartment Ivan had built there. So it turned out that the Reeder family had members living in Shaniko from 1885 until 1960, when Ivan closed the only store in town and John Reeder and his family moved to Portland. Mary died March 3, 1981.

After finishing school in Portland, Teresa returned to Central Oregon to teach three years in Kent, and again had the sadness of being displaced at the end of an era because school at Kent was discontinued and the children were transported to Grass Valley. She lives in Portland.

Marguerite Reeder, the youngest child in the family, was born July 10, 1916. In grade school she won first prize in the foot race at the Wasco County track meet in Tygh Valley. She graduated from Shaniko High School in 1934 along with Phyllis Hanna (Hess) in the last class to graduate from Shaniko. She attended Behnke-Walker Business College in Portland. When the Second World War came, she and her

Marguerite Reeder won first prize in the foot race at the Wasco County Fair. She was employed in the County Assessor's office later.

niece, Teresa Jones, worked in the shipyards. She and her husband, Clarence Starr, moved to Albany to operate Elma and Lg's restaurant. She retired, then worked in the county assessor's office. Marguerite died July 27, 1981.

## William Arthur Rees
## January 1, 1871-May 7, 1955

Bill Rees, son of David Rees and Sarah Thomas of Glanswyth, Wales, grew up in Llandilo, Carmarthenshire. The signs "Go West Young Man, Go West!" were appearing in Wales when Bill was 21 and he decided to go see the American West. He asked his father for a share of the family estate and shipped out of Liverpool in 1893 on the USS *Scythia*, bound for Boston, Massachusetts, then took the train to Helmsville, Montana, to see his cousin Harry Rees. Not liking the cold weather in Montana, he left for Oregon, where he homesteaded the lower half of Rabbit Island in the Columbia River about six miles above The Dalles. Commercial salmon fishing was common up and down the river, with large catches being made, but at that time there was little market for the catch; prices were very low. It was a lonely life. The only way to reach the island was by small boat, so he leased his land and moved to The Dalles. Moody Warehouse hired the young immigrant as bookkeeper and in 1900 sent him to the growing town of Shaniko.

A letter written to his father in Wales right after he arrived in The Dalles gives Bill Rees's first impression of the Far West in The Dalles area:

The Dalles, Ore.
Dec. 31, 1893

Dear Father:

Having a few hours to spare I take up my pen to tell you about the far West. I left Montana early in November and went out further about 700 miles. The climate here is far superior to that of Montana. I could just sit out all day and not feel cold.

The farmers depend chiefly on wheat and owing to a wet autumn, thousands of bushels have been spoiled and is of no use except for pig feed. Pig raising is the trade that pays best. You can get the best wheat at 30c a bushel, so you can guess that the farmers are rather down hearted at present, but they expect a good crop next summer.

You will get hardly anything for horses. I saw two good young horses sold the other day for $10 apiece. Cattle are dearer than horses, about $25 for a good three-year-old steer and about $15 for fat cows. Beef is dearer than mutton. Plenty of sheep. No more news, wishing you a happy Christmas and prosperous New Year.

Your affectionate son
William

Bill was a connoisseur of humor. He found some amusing twist to almost every situation in life. English is the second

language in Wales and Bill's schooling was primarily conducted in English, but he told this story about his arrival
in Boston, "When I got off the ship I was hungry and tried
to communicate my need for food by pointing to my mouth.
Before I could make myself understood I was in a dentist
chair and three teeth had been pulled."

He poked fun at the British and Americans without fear or
favor, sitting for hours at a time regaling visitors to Shaniko
with one joke after another from a seemingly inexhaustible
supply. One of his favorite jokes concerned the visiting
Englishman who inquired, "What do you mean, you 'can'
things?" He was told, "We eat what garden produce we can,
and what we can't eat, we can." This appealed to the
Englishman who then wrote home, "These people here eat
what they can, and what they can't eat, they put up in little
tin boxes, don't you know."

Bill enjoyed a play on sounds when telling an anecdote.
If he was reminded of his visit to Montana he sometimes
would say plaintively, "I wa-a-a-a-ant to go ba-a-a-ack to
Monta-a-a-a-a-na!" making it sound like the bleating of a
sheep, since much of Montana was sheep-grazing country
when he was there.

The Rees home was built on lots one and two in block 11.
The house grew with the family—another bedroom at the
back, a screened porch on the west, a cellar to store canned
goods, and finally two small houses to the south, built
and occupied by Harry and Jack Rees, when the main house
became crowded.

Bill Rees found his niche in Shaniko and was completely
contented there. He never returned to Wales. His position
at the warehouse kept him in touch with the farmers, stockmen, and townspeople. He took an active part in civic
affairs, serving on the town council most of the years he lived
in Shaniko. In all of these affairs he was known for his
integrity. Being a Welshman, he loved to sing. When the
Rees children and grandchildren were small he sang whimsi-

cal songs like the one he called, "Peeping through the Knothole in Grandpa's Wooden Leg." The townschildren loved to sit around him while he regaled them with stories he made up on the spot. When he had grandchildren he would cradle one on each arm of his favorite big chair while one sat on his knees and others leaned against his legs. The stories they loved best were about people named Flannery, Haggerty, and McKelvey. The plots centered around the family pets Patsy the terrier, and Topsy the shetland pony. He also played the cornet in the local band.

By 1942 it became hard for him to see to keep books so he sold the warehouses to his long-time employee Frank Wagner, and spent the last years quietly at home making the daily trip to the post office with a stop-off at the hotel to pass the time of day and tell a joke or two. The first time he was ever admitted to a hospital was three days before he died, at Prineville General Hospital.

## Lillie May McHargue Rees
## (April 20, 1875-March 8, 1968)

Lillie or "Lil" McHargue was born in Brownsville, Oregon, of pioneer parents James McHargue and Emma Keeney. The family moved to Washington, then back to Albany where Lil received her education. When she was 26 (1901) she and her sister Jane and cousin Ilene Keeney went to Shaniko, where Lil worked as head waitress for her uncle James Keeney in the Columbia Southern Hotel.

Jane, Ilene Keeney, Elizabeth Matlock and Lil took up a timber culture in Crook County on land at Agency Plains, signing papers before Commissioner Bell in Prineville, July 30, 1903, the same· day that J.W. Fisher and James Keeney signed such papers. The young women planned to build a house on the intersection of their claims, with each having

Bill Rees followed the signs in Glanswyth, Wales, saying "Go West, Young Man, Go West".

Bill Rees arrived in Shaniko in 1900 to bid on wool for Moody Warehouse Co. of The Dalles. He returned in 1901 and lived the rest of his life there. He eventually owned the warehouses.

Lillie Rees "gave of herself to her community, not seeking joy nor feeling pain, but as the myrtle breathes forth its fragrance into space—from behind the eyes of such as these, God speaks—and smiles upon the earth." (Gilbran)

Adelbert and Harry Rees went to the City Park in Portland on their way to Brownsville to spend the summer.

her bedroom on her own land, thus proving up on their claims and living together too.

Bill Rees and Lillie McHargue took the train to Portland where they were married April 5, 1903, in the home of her parents. They raised four sons, Adelbert, Harry, Jack, and Jimmy, and one daughter, Lillian Margaret, who married Ivan Olsen. Their grandaughter, little Margaret, was raised by her grandparents because her mother died of childbirth.

Lillie Rees was a practical woman who knew how to paper the house, raise a fine garden, can and preserve food for the family, prepare wonderful meals for anyone who was lonely or stopped at their home as they were traveling through. She kept a well-stocked cupboard. Sewing supplies were at hand to make Red Cross garments or fill a missionary box. When it was evening and the radio was turned on, she sat across the heater from her husband; but her hands were not idle even then, for she was mending or doing needlework until bedtime. Her life brings to mind the words of Kahlil Gibran in *The Prophet*, "And there are those who give and know not pain in giving, nor do they seek joy, nor give with mindfulness of virtue. They give as in yonder valley the myrtle breathes it fragrance into space. Through the hands of such as these God speaks, and from behind their eyes He smiles upon the earth."

After Bill died, Mrs. Rees lived most of the nine years left of her life with sons' and granddaughter's families. She died in San Diego while visiting Margaret. The Rev. John Richardson, who had spent many days in the Rees home, read from Proverbs 31 at her last rites at St. Paul's Episcopal Church in The Dalles:

A wife of noble character is hard to find, she is worth more than rubies
Her husband has full confidence in her and lacks nothing of value.
She brings him good, not harm all the days of her life.

She selects wool and flax and works with eager hands.
She gets up while it is still dark; she provides food for
her family.
She sets about her work vigorously; her arms are strong
for her task.

She opens her arms to the poor and extends her hands
to the needy.
When it snows, she has no fear for her household, for
all are clothed with scarlet
She speaks with wisdom, and faithful instruction is on
her tongue.

Her children arise and call her blessed; her husband
also praises her.
Many women do noble things, but you surpass them all.

This passage from the Bible epitomizes the life of Lillie Rees.

## William Adelbert Rees
### December 19, 1904

Adelbert, first son of Bill and Lillie Rees, was born in
Portland. He started school in September before his sixth
birthday under the direction of Louise Rintoul. At the time
he was in grade school there were two rooms in the school
building. In 1919 another room was added at the back of the
schoolhouse for high school classes. He completed high
school in three years, graduating in 1921 at age 16. His exposure to learning in the greater halls of knowledge took
place that fall at Oregon Agricultural College (now Oregon
State University) in Corvallis. That exposure didn't "take"
and he returned to Shaniko at the end of his first term.

Back home he worked with the county crew grading dirt
roads, then for Jim Fisher during haying for $1.99 a day (one

Left: on March 1, 1954, Dwight Eisenhower appointed Adelbert Rees postmaster of Fairview, Oregon. Right: Helen Guyton Rees, age 17.

The couple made their home in a small cottage across the street from the Moody house.

Adelbert and Helen Rees celebrated the 50th anniversary of their marriage (1929-1979). From left to right: Glade Steinmetz, James Rees, Irma Rees, Richard Nelson, Harry and Maye Rees. Back row: Adelbert and Helen, Margaret Nelson, Volna and Pearl Guyton (brother of Helen, and his wife).

Four children were born to Adelbert and Helen Rees. Front row, from left: Anna Bell, Bill, Dick, Charles.

The grown and married family of Adelbert and Helen Rees, from left: Barbara and husband Bill Rees, son Charles and wife Patricia, daughter Anna Bell and husband Hal Rosene, Helen and Adelbert, Sandra and husband Dick Rees.

cent off for Workman's Compensation) and finally at the Farmer's Elevator for a short time before going to work for Moody Warehouse. He remained a regular employee there.

On the anniversary of Bill and Clara Moody's wedding, January 4, 1929, Adelbert Rees and Helen Guyton, daughter of Will C. and Ada Bell Guyton, were married at the ranch home of the bride's parents between Shaniko and Kent. They took up residence in a small house John McHargue had remodeled just across the street from the Moody residence.

At that time Shaniko was a fairly busy village with a bank, hotel, good store, daily trains, and large warehouses filled with wool, wheat, hay, and other commodities such as wood, lumber, kerosene, and coal.

There was quite a business community with a social life as well. In early 1929 Wall Street was having the jitters, but Shaniko was not feeling it yet.

The ladies met for afternoon bridge and couples exchanged evening party or dinner invitations. These were nice affairs with flowered centerpieces on white linens and food served with sterling silver. The 19th Amendment was in force, so liquid refreshments consisted of coffee, tea, and punch.

Week-end dances were usual, either in Shaniko or one of the nearby towns. The 19th Amendment was *not* in effect at *these* affairs—unless there was a raid. The liquid refreshments consumed outside the dance halls were not percolated in the kitchen, but in the still out on the hills. Many people enjoyed dancing without ever seeing a flask or tasting moonshine; but there were those who patronized the dances because moonshine was available outside.

Four chilldren were born to the Adelbert Rees family during their residence in Shaniko: William Robert "Bill" (1931), Richard Harry "Dick" (1935), Anna Bell (1937), and Charles Arthur (1938).

During the 13 years the family lived in Shaniko the Depression had settled in, the bank had closed, and most social life had tapered away to a trickle. The highway had been improved and Shaniko, like most of the Sherman County towns, saw business going to The Dalles. The warehouses were losing the business of the farmers who were building bulk grain storage at home and hauling their own grain to market. The train made three runs a week to Shaniko, and finally came only when there was a carload lot of grain or stock to be shipped.

Students at school averaged eight or ten.

Then came the Second World War!

By this time Bill Rees was ready to retire. He sold the warehouses, opening the way for Adelbert to move his family where there were better schools and work. In August 1942 the family moved to Fairview, Oregon, and Adelbert began work for the Union Pacific Railroad as watchman for the switch engine serving the newly constructed Reynolds

Metals Aluminum Plant near Troutdale. When that job ended he worked for Les Walrad in Gresham and then at the box factory there. On March 1, 1954, President Dwight Eisenhower appointed him Postmaster of Fairview, a position he held for over 21 years. He retired in 1975.

The Adelbert Rees children grew up in Fairview and graduated from Gresham High School.

William Robert became an Episcopal priest. His wife, May Jo Wyman, and he had three children: Robert William, May Jo, and Rachel Elizabeth. His wife died when the children were young. Presently he is married to Barbara Winder. She has four grown children, Rex, Brad, Joan, and Scott. The Reeses live at Shady Cove.

Richard Harry's wife is Sandra Crosser. Dick is a steel worker in the Long Beach area. Their sons, Dan Clifford and Stephen Edward, are both out of high school.

Anna Bell married Hal Rosene and both are schoolteachers with their home in Boring. Their eldest is Cynthia Lee who attended University of Oregon and Daniel who completed his sophomore year at University of Portland.

Charles Arthur is professor of law at the University of Baltimore Law School and his wife Patricia is a teacher in their home city of Columbia, Maryland. Their daughters Emily and Elizabeth attend school in Columbia.


## Lillian Margaret Rees
### May 7, 1906-May 23, 1930

Lillian Margaret "Peggy" was born at a time when doctors were not required to put drops in the eyes of newborn infants as they are now. Because of this omission, Peggy was almost blind her first two years and lived with her grandmother McHargue in Portland under the care of an eye specialist. After that, periodically it was necessary for her to

Margaret Rees graduated with the second high school class. She died in childbirth. Her parents raised her infant, "Little Margaret." Right: W.A. Rees and Little Margaret.

Left: The W.A. Rees children Adelbert, Harry, Jimmy, Jack, Margaret, 1914. Right: Margaret Olsen graduated from Maupin High School.

go to Portland for more treatments. She was away from home much of the time until she finished high school. Clara Moody, who was living alone following her husband's death, loved Peggy and liked to have her come after school and spend the night with her. Mrs. Moody supervised her practice and gave her piano lessons. After she was grown, Margaret took jazz piano lessons and became a fine jazz player.

She attended Oregon Agricultural College one term, then returned home and went to work at Gavin-Wheeler Company as part-time bookkeeper. Ivan Olsen also worked in the store.

Ivan played the saxophone and the two formed a small dance band with Sonny Spalinger playing the drums. They made $10 an evening each—big money in those days.

Ivan and Peggy were going many places together by this time. One evening she was to spend the night with Mrs. Moody, so her parents didn't look for her home after work. The next morning Mrs. Moody came to see why she hadn't arrived the night before. It was soon learned that Ivan was away, also, and they had decided the two may have run away to get married. Her parents found a note verifying their assuption and were pretty upset. Bride and groom returned in time to go back to work Monday morning.

Playing for Saturday night dances occupied their week-ends the first months after their marriage. In May, 1930, Peggy went to The Dalles to await the arrival of their child. She stayed with Marion Lord, Wasco County Health Nurse and friend of the family. The evening of the twenty-second of May, she entered the hospital. Before midnight she gave birth to a six-pound baby girl who was later named Lillian Margaret for her mother. By 2 p.m. the next day, Peggy was dead. No autopsy was performed and it was not determined what caused such sudden death to a healthy mother, though it was believed to have been a postpartum infection.

Two weeks later "Little Margaret" was taken to the home of her Rees grandparents and lived with them until after her graduation from high school at Maupin.

Across the street from the Rees residence, Glade and Wayne McCulloch soon took up residence at the Shell Station and Restaurant. Their daughter, Mary Ada "Pat," just two months older than Little Margaret, soon became a regular companion and friend of Little Margaret. The girls attended grade school in Shaniko, and their first two years of high school in Moro, then went to Maupin.

After graduation Margaret attended business college in Portland and worked in the city a number of years before moving to California. She married Terry Nelson. Their son, Richard Nelson, 23, is in the Navy; with his wife Amy and daughter Lori he lives in San Diego. The Nelsons' daughter Wendy lives in Ramona, California, and the Nelsons at El Cajon.

## Harry Alfred Rees

Harry Alfred Rees was born in Portland, December 18, 1907. When about a year old he was baptized by Bishop Paddock.

In 1922 a class of three graduated from Shaniko High School; Margaret Logan, Clarence Fisk, and Harry Rees. Mr. Charles B. Roe was principal.There was nothing in town for a 15-year-old graduate to do, so the next year he took post-graduate classes. Clyde Bonney was principal that year. The students from surrounding towns who came to Shaniko with him made up the largest class ever to graduate from Shaniko. Harry's sister Margaret was among the ten graduates.

He worked for his father in the warehouse several years. In the fall of 1928 a car accident caused a stiffness in his leg, so he went to Portland and enrolled at Behnke-Walker Business College, to study bookkeeping. His first job was for True-Blue Biscuit Company, and he remained with the company in Portland and Seattle until he retired in 1970.

Rees brothers from left: Adelbert, James, Harry.

On October 24, 1931, he married Maxine, daughter of a pharmacist, Roland D. Jackson, and his wife Alma. After their family was grown, they separated. Maxine, now retired, lives in Portland. She is a graduate of Immaculata Catholic High School in Portland. Their children, James A., Shirley Ann, and Mary Jo, were all born in Portland.

On May 27, 1965 James A. married Sharon Lea DuBois of Bradford, Pa. They have three sons, Douglas, Robert, and Bradford; all live in Portland.

Shirley and Jack Eyler married, Nov. 25, 1961. They make Bellevue, Washington, home, with children Craig, Kathleen, Thomas, Susan and Teresa.

Left: Harry Rees was associated with Tru Blu Biscuit Company until he retired. Of his Salmon catch he said, "I caught a 23-pound, 9½-ounce salmon. I knew the exact weight because I checked its scales." Right: Jack Rees entered the Second World War with a rank of Lt. (jg) and after the war remained working in Washington, D.C., standardizing equipment used by the Navy and Army Air Force (late U.S. Air Force).

The Harry Rees family, at the time of the marriage of their daughter, Shirley Anne. From left: Harry, his wife Maxine, the bride Shirley, her sister Mary Jo, and her brother James A. Rees.

On May 20, 1961, Mary Jo and Kennth DeWall married. They live in Seattle with children, Shaun, Brian, and Aimee.

Harry has hobbies which bring him plenty of satisfaction. He tells of catching his largest salmon, a 35-pounder at Juneau, Alaska, and a 23-pound-9½ ounce salmon at Westport. "I knew the exact weight of the latter," he said, "because I checked its scales."

"Bowling?" he asked, "I have 10 or 12 trophies." Mary Jo bowled with him several years. Their team won trophies for being the first place winner for the year. He says he will quit bowling when he picks up the 7-10 split and when he bowls a 300 game—which means he'll bowl as long as he can, for those events will never occur.

Since retiring he has taken several part-time bookkeeping jobs, one of which was with Carolyn Hansen Fashion College. "Real nice place to work," said Harry. "Some beautiful women there too, though I am so busy I hardly have time to notice them!"

Harry and his present wife, Maye Kyllonen, make their home in N. Seattle. Maye is a talented artist. She enjoys numerous hobbies as well.

## John Robert "Jack" Rees
## June 19, 1911

One of the first memories of Jack Rees was making the trip from his grandmother's home in Portland to The Dalles on the sternwheeler, accompanied by his uncle John McHargue. He loved watermelon and by the time they docked at The Dalles he was sick and they missed the train to Shaniko—so stayed at The Dalles Hotel. A very exciting trip for a small child! Another event that impressed him was the day his father drove home a 1921 model "big-six" Stude-

Left: Jack and Helen Juliana Biedron were married in 1951. The two young people often hiked the Appalachian Trails. Right: Jack and Helen had one daughter, Frances.

baker touring car with jump seats to accomodate seven passengers.

Jack graduated from Oregon State College in 1934 with a degree in Mechanical Engineering. It was during the Depression and few jobs were available. He eventually got work at the Puget Sound Navy Yard in Bremerton, Washington. In 1943 he entered the Navy with rank of Lt. (jg) and ended up in Washington D.C., working in an office whose purpose was to implement the standardization of equipment used by the Navy and Army Air Force (later the US Airforce). When the war ended he stayed in the same office, doing similar work as a civilian. In 1956 he transferred to the National Bureau of Standards and worked there until his retirement in 1970.

He and Helen Juliana Biedron were married in 1951. Helen is the daughter of John Biedron and Rose Radlinski of Farnow, Poland, who married after immigrating to Chicago where Helen was born. The two young people often hiked on the Appalachian Trail in Virginia. 'Their daughter Frances Stephanie was born in March 1957. She graduated from the College of Mount St. Joseph in Ohio in 1978.

Soon after Jack and Helen were married they bought a farm near Woodbridge, Virginia and lived there until Jack retired, then moved to Williamsburg, Va.

## James Angus Rees
## January 23, 1913

"I was the only one of the Rees tribe born in Shaniko," Jim said, "the only logical explanation for choosing Shaniko being that I wished to be near my mother." Louise Rintoul was a sponsor at his baptism in Shaniko in 1913, and the certificate was signed by Charles H. Powell.

Jimmy went through 12 grades in the Shaniko School, graduating alone in 1930. The 50th anniversary of that event he said there was a class reunion, And, as has been the case for the last 49, there was a 100 percent turnout."

Jim worked summers for Jim Fisher, and for his father in the warehouse a while before enrolling at Behnke-Walker Business College, considered the best such school in Portland. He returned to Shaniko to work in lambing at the Fisher Ranch until the college called him to come take a book-keeping job at the North Portland Stockyards. He took the job and lived at the Exchange Hotel.

After Pearl Harbor the Army notified him to sign up for service, April 2, 1942. He was sent to Monterey, Fort Ord, Marysville, and finally, to Goff's, California, for desert maneuvers. He sailed on the *Sibonet* to land at Casa Blanca. With Graves Registration he crossed the northwest corner of Africa and traveled to Sicily, across the straights of Messina to the toe of Italy, then up through Rome and up to the fighting, then back to Naples. His platoon went into southern France, always following the fighting—but keeping a respectful distance behind. They were picking up dead soldiers and were told that there wasn't much sense in adding to the count.

Left: Jim Rees became Pvt. 1st Class in the Army Graves Registration and served in North Africa, Sicily, Italy, and France. Right: Jim Rees came home on furlough and "swept the beauteous Irma McPherson off her feet," he said, and married her before returning to Europe. "It wasn't long until the war was over, but it seemed like it was."

"I came home on furlough," he said, "arriving in Portland, Janaury 10, where I swept the beauteous Irma McPherson off her feet and married her January 25th, then headed back to Europe on Valentine's Day. The war didn't last much longer—though it seemed like it did—and I was discharged October 10, 1945."

He returned to the stockyards and worked in North Portland until his retirement in 1975.

The wife of Jim Rees was Irma Lucile McPherson, born September 11, 1914, at Emmett, Idaho, to Mr. and Mrs. Ross A. McPherson. Her grandfather McPherson started the first school in Harney County, Oregon, and maintained active interest and participation in the school system all his life. A teacher and minister, he was performing the duties of County School Superintendent in Ontario, Oregon, when he died.

Irma's mother, Mary E. Sheperd, also came from a pioneering family, since her father was one of the first freighters between Walla Walla and Umatilla, and into Idaho.

When Irma was small her parents moved to Portland where she attended St. Helen's Hall, majoring in music. She was organist at Kenton United Presbyterian Church several years. Before her marraige she was employed by Clark, Taylor & Hoard Comm. Co. in North Portland. When their children were grown she worked for the Portland School District at Grant High School. She is retired.

Children of the James Rees family are John, born June 21, 1947, a graduate of Cornell I. in engineering and of Harvard Business School. He is general manager of the Oregon Region for Quadrant, a subsidiary of Weyerhaeuser. In 1977 he married Patricia Cunerty. Sarabeth was born in 1978.

Mary Anne, daughter of James Rees and his wife Irma, was born on John's fifth birthday (1952), received a master's degree in music from Indiana U. and is assistant Professor of Music at Willamette U., presently on leave of absence to study for her doctorate at the University of Oregon.

## John Reid

John Reid was a garageman in Shaniko. In about 1928 he tore down what had been the Townsite Building, attached to the Columbia Southern Hotel, and built a garage and house where it had stood. The Reids lived there until about 1940.

John bought an old engine which had a huge flywheel, put a belt on it, and connected it with a generator to make electricity to light his buildings, the school house, and the Moody house. This was the one source of electricity in Shaniko at the time. It was wonderful to have electric lights, even if the service was liable to be erratic. When the plant was stopped the lights gradually faded out; fortunately, there was time to light a kerosene lamp before the room was plunged in darkness.

## Family of William Reinhart

Bill Reinhart and Daisy Bell Warner were married in Indiana. He was in Shaniko operating Hotel Shaniko in 1902. Four children were born to the couple. The first child was Teresa Dolores (April 21, 1900-1958). After they began living on his homestead a child was stillborn. He had a pet goat, usually tethered, but one day, in December 1904, Mrs. Reinhart went out to hang out clothes, not knowing the goat was loose, and he caught her unaware. She was nearly due to deliver her second child. The goat butted her repeatedly, knocking her down. Three days later she gave birth to a baby boy stillborn. Mrs. Reinhart was quite ill for some time as a result of her injuries.

A boy, Joseph Cleo, arrived January 22, 1906 (died 1971). In 1908 Reinhart was running the Palace, a rooming house with butcher shop adjoining, when Celia Helena was born, August 3. Some of the men at the rooming house had never seen a newborn baby, so her father took them upstairs to watch his wife bathe her.

After the big fire in 1911 which burned all the hotels and rooming houses except the Columbia Southern Hotel, the Reinharts moved to The Dalles, then to Wasco, where he operated the Club Saloon until Oregon went dry. From there the family went into the restaurant business in Ashland with a Mr. Taylor, making bread with lithia water, a natural mineral water found there.

During World War I Reinhart served hot chili to the Mexican section hands, made from a recipe he bought at Shaniko for $25. He set tables out on the sidewalk in front of the pool hall and restaurant he was managing near the depot, and put cups of cherries and other fruits out for the troops who got off the trains going through. Things began being difficult for the Reinhart family because he was German. When some women accused Mrs. Reinhart of being

Bill and Daisy Bell Reinhart came to Shaniko in 1902. He operated Hotel Shaniko, then the Palace Saloon.

Mr. and Mrs. Reinhart and children (front row, to right of post).

Left: Reinhart children Celia, Delores and Joseph. Right: When Delores was small there was a baby popularity contest which she won. The prize was a beautiful doll with long curls, still beautiful years after Delores is gone. Picture taken in 1982.

pro-German, "The fight was on," and the Reinhart family moved to Sacramento. It was a terrible trip over the narrow dirt roads, crossing the mountains in the pouring rain.

That winter the big flu epidemic reached the West. The Reinharts were living in a six-unit apartment house. Someone died in every unit but theirs. When the Armistice was signed Reinhart got an "extra" in the middle of the night, telling the news. The next day the family joined the celebrating crowds downtown.

They moved back to Ashland where Dolores married her Ashland sweetheart, Cecil Norton, when he returned from France. Their children were Margaret and William. Joe never married. He was an architect and draftsman, but joined the "Seabees" and was on Guadalcanal during the worst of the fighting there. The unit received a Presidential Citation. After the war he had a shop in Portland, where he died in 1971.

Celia became a nurse in San Francisco. She married James Franklin Hays in 1928. She first met him in Ashland when they were third graders. Jim worked for Standard Oil for 35 years. He died in 1968.

William Reinhart feared the black lung disease of his youth might return, but his death came about in 1943 as the result of an injury he received when he was struck by a boxcar which had been shunted alone down the railroad track without warning.

Mrs. Reinhart lived to be a month short of 95 years, active until her last illness with pneumonia—baking cakes and crotcheting afghans.


## William E. Rhodes, Depot Agent

William E. Rhodes was born in one of the northeastern states. He came to Shaniko in 1927 as depot agent for the Union Pacific RR Co. His wife, Nella, was born in Georgia. Her father was a carpenter. He taught her his trade. She used this skill to advantage wherever she lived. In Shaniko she remodeled the depot—moved partitions and the stairway and built cupboards in the kitchen.

The Rhodes family enjoyed dancing and bridge, so joined the social activities of the community. They had no children. From Shaniko they moved to Blalock, Biggs and The Dalles. While living in The Dalles they built a home and became Episcopalians.

When Bill Rhodes retired from the railroad, the couple moved to the retirement village of Ryderwood, Washington. Within a few years Bill died of cancer and Nella remained in the community, remodeling houses and exchanging them for those needing work—until she bought a house just outside of Ryderwood proper. She isolated herself from most of her friends the last few years of her life and lived pretty much as a recluse. She was taken to a hospital and then a rest home where she died. The authorities did not know where she should be buried, nor did her friends know when she died until letters were returned to them, months after her burial. Still more months later, her brother, located in Georgia, presumably had her remains moved to rest beside her husband, Bill Rhodes, in the Vader Cemetery.

## Louise Rintoul, Shaniko Teacher
### 1864-1955

Miss Louise Rintoul was born of pioneer parents living in The Dalles. Her father, Robert Rintoul, was a Scotsman born in 1825; her mother, Mary, also born in 1825, came from the Isle of Man. They came west from Alabama by covered wagon.

Louise attended grade school with Will Guyton at Jap Hollow near The Dalles. When she completed the grade school "books," she taught him and others during several terms before she finished her education and began teaching fourth grade in The Dalles school. From there she went to Shaniko to teach for about six years, then to Milton-Free-water and Weston, Oregon. Miss Louise was "born to teach." Children loved her, and all her associations with them turned into memorable learning experiences for them.

She boarded and roomed at the Columbia Southern Hotel until the influx of workers on the railroad up the Deschutes made it so crowded at the hotel that she was asked to room elsewhere; she continued to eat at the hotel. It was a regular arrangement for her and Tom Gavin to eat meals at the same table; both were single and they enjoyed each other's company. Neither ever married. Miss Rintoul roomed at the Rees home the rest of her stay in Shaniko; the friendship lasted for life.

In 1935 she retired at 70 and moved to Portland. She lived to be 91, her memory clear, her interest in people unabated, though her eyesight failed the last two years.

## James Robertson, Sr.

James Robertson was born in Scotland. He ran a transfer and delivery business in Antelope before moving to Shaniko, where he kept a large livery barn. He delivered feed, coal, and wood in both towns for many years.

## Children of James Robertson, Sr.

1. Peter "Pete" herded sheep a while, then ran the Shaniko Pastime. He lived most of his life around Shaniko.

2. Margaret "Maggie' married Alec McLennan. At one time she and her husband ran the Columbia Southern Hotel. They moved to Bend and continued in the hotel business. Their children: Aileen, Edward, and Catherine.

3. James "Jimmy" packed for herders a while, then lived in Shaniko. Jimmy loved to hunt. He and Charley McCutcheon often hunted together. Jimmy married Agnes Kaser Tatum, who had one child, Robert Tatum. Jimmy was for a time foreman of the State Highway Maintenance crew based in Shaniko. Robert Tatum married Geraldine Norton of Kent and farms near Kent.

## Children of Gus and Antonia Schmidt

Gus Schmidt, an early settler at Cross Hollows, and his wife, Antonia Eastkraut Schmidt, had eight children: Armand,

Agnes, Hattie, Max, Ernest, Otto, Arthur, and Lucille.

Armand lost his sight when about ten. He and his sister, Agnes, used to get in the huge wool sacks to stomp the wool down during shearing. When he was 14 his parents sent him to Germany with Antonia's brother, Julius Eastkraut, hoping medical care would restore his sight. He returned to Cross Hollows when he was about 17, still blind.

Agnes went to St. Mary's Catholic School in The Dalles. She married Otto Frederick Hinkle of Anna, Illinois. For a time he worked on ranches, then was employed in the railroad yards at The Dalles. He later became a fireman, then engineer on the Shaniko line. The family maintained a home in The Dalles. He died about 1940. Mrs. Hinkle lives in The Dalles. Their children are Ernest and Dorothy.

Hattie also attended St. Mary's before her marriage to Charles Spitzer. They moved to Chicago. Their daughters, Helen and Margaret, accompanied her when she returned to Oregon. He remained in Chicago. Later, Hattie married Arch Hanna, the stepson of Jim Stark. Children born to Hattie and Arch were Lois and Billy.

Max married Bernice DeGroot of Antelope. They live in Mosier.

Ernest married the widow of Bonney Duus.

Otto went to Alaska to fish. His two sons live there.

Arthur and his wife, Gladys Peters, had one son, Donald. The family lived at Ridgeway. Arthur was a rancher. Donald left Central Oregon to live in the Willamette Valley. Arthur married again. He died later.

Lucille was seven-month baby weighing 2½ pounds at birth, which apparently did not affect her health as she and her husband, Carl Thompson, lived to celebrate their golden wedding anniversary. They have two sons, Fred and Arthur, and one daughter. The Dalles is their home.

Frank Wagner arrived in Shaniko in 1910. He worked in the Moody Warehouse until 1942 when he bought out Bill Rees. At that time he also owned the Farmer's Elevator.

## Frank Phillip Wagner

Frank Phillip Wagner was born May 23, 1888, in Arthur, North Dakota, worked as a boy in the local elevator, then attended Minnesota University. For five years before coming to Shaniko in 1910, he had been employed in the bank in Arthur. On arrival in Shaniko, he went to work in the Moody Warehouse, and while he did other things at particular times, he was employed there until he bought the warehouses from Bill Rees in 1942.

On July 4, 1917, the community had a party for Walter Beyer and Frank Wagner before they left for the Army. Of his service in the Army in 1918, Frank said:

I was in the Infantry, 77th Division, served in "The Argonne." I was in the Army about a year, most of the time in France. Our division was "Up Front" in trenches a few months. We were retreating, starting to lose the line. The lieutenat told me, "Frank, you'll have to go ahead and draw fire." You could hear shells coming, a sizzling noise.

When the men asked what protection they would have, they were ordered to "get out there and take it!" He said, "I came home June, 1918, got the flu after arriving home."

Frank had a homestead in Thorn Hollow on the Bakeoven road. Even though he had a team and wagon, he preferred to walk to Shaniko to work...about four miles. After he returned from France, Frank lived in a room in the north warehouse across from the Rees residence. Later he lived in a room in the south end of the big warehouse.

When the Altermatts left Shaniko, Frank bought their home, remodeled it and lived the rest of his Shaniko years there.

Frank Wagner was a 68-year-old bachelor when he met and married the Shaniko schoolteacher, Myrtle Ryden. They lived several years in Shaniko, but when Frank sold the warehouses and elevator, they moved to Portland.

On Tuesday, May 23, 1978, friends of Frank Wagner gathered at the Adelbert Rees home in Fairview to honor him on his 90th birthday. All of the sons and daughters of Gus Reeder were present...Tommy and Elsie Jones and their daughter came from Dufur for the occasion. Just after his 91st birthday one year later, Frank Wagner died.

## George Ward

George Ward was born in Antelope, Oregon, February 2, 1914, the only son of Thomas Chester "Tom" and Mary Good. Tom Ward was a photographer who came from around Pendleton to Antelope. He furnished the horses and equipment for building the Old Antelope Road, planted the orchard in the canyon, and built the old cistern which supplied water for the City of Antelope. He died in Antelope and was buried there in about 1926.

When he was about ten or eleven years old, young George remembers going with his father to haul wheat to Shaniko.

Tom drove a six-horse team and George drove four horses. He particularly remembers the sound of empty wheat wagons, brakes set, squealing down the old Antelope grade.

"I went to school and worked for Omar Borthwick on his place above Antelope," said George. "I milked seventeen cows night and morning for two-bits a day."

He married Mary Hampton of The Dalles. Their children are Eric and Joan. Eric is now farming part of the Ward land. Water is plentiful in the valley where the Wards occupy what was the Hinton Ranch. There the lawns are green and a swimming pool invites a cool dip on a hot day. Mary Hampton Ward died in October, 1970.

George Ward claims three grown foster children; Mrs. Grover Starr, Mrs. Ray Horton, and Kelly Mitchell.

A new home was built beside the large original ranch house. In 1973 Ward married Bobbie Burns (Shaver).

Talking about his ranching operations George said, "When moving the cattle from one pasture to another it was necessary to cross the highway. That presented no problem for most of the animals—except a roan steer they called Roany, who shied when he was driven to the yellow line, stalled, then turned and bolted for home. They let him go, but each year it was the same story. When he reached that yellow line it was some kind of danger signal to him, and off he'd snort for the canyon. They finally had to haul him out on a truck so he wouldn't have to bring himself to step over that fatal yellow line, but by that time he weighed a ton."

George Ward has been active in the work of the Wheat League, Wool Growers Association, and the Cattlemen's Association. In spite of poor health much of the recent two years, he is only semi-retired.

Alma Werner was a nurse caring for San Francisco earthquake victims before coming to Oregon. She married Charles Werner; together they and their son, Eugene, arrived with a wagonload of lumber to build their homestead cabin.

# Alma Grossman Werner
## April 18, 1880-August 7, 1964

Alma Grossman was born in Waverly, Iowa. Because of the poor health of her father who farmed some distance from Waverly, Alma lived in town with her grandparents and went to school. Her grandfather was the German founder and preacher of a private young men's college in Waverly. Alma suffered from something similar to Parkinson's disease as a girl. Her family hoped that learning to play the piano might help control the trembling. She loved the music and learned to play well, but she never overcame the tremors.

Alma also studied nursing. At the time of the earthquake in San Francisco she cared for the injured in an outdoor emergency hospital.

Some friends of hers were coming to Oregon and she accompanied them. While visiting in the state she met and married Charles Werner. Their only child, Eugene, was small when his parents took up a homestead around 1915, located east and north of Bakeoven near the Hinton-Ward Place. The Werner Family arrived in Shaniko loaded with the lumber for their homestead cabin which they built on the hill. Alma carried water from a shallow spring in the canyon. She built a catch basin and related that the spring filled slowly (at the rate of about a bucket an hour). While she waited for the spring to refill, she was frightened of the rattlesnakes, fearing for her own safety as well as that of Eugene, who always accompanied her. The yellow jackets were bad too, and she had to go to the spring early in the morning or late in the evening to avoid being stung. Charles worked for Hinton while they lived on the homestead.

When Eugene was old enough to attend school, the Werners moved to Shaniko and lived in a house on which Alma did much of the building and finishing work. After they moved to Shaniko, Charley managed the Farmer's Elevator.

The Werners separated in 1930 and Charles left Shaniko. Mrs. Werner maintained her home there the rest of her active life. She taught music to succeeding generations of children, imparting wisdom and inspiration along with her music. She was a well-loved member of the community. Her English was fair, but people who understood the German language said Alma spoke classic German.

Her son, Eugene, joined the Civilian Conservation Corps during the Great Depression. His group worked at Camp Friend (near the community of Friend, Ore.) above Dufur for six months, then spent five months at Camp Benson (near Waukena Falls). After he returned home, one day he took his mother for a Sunday outing. She fell and broke her hip. After a month in the hospital, Alma returned to Shaniko. Mrs. Reeder took care of her until she was able to return home. The injury to her hip never fully healed. The rest of her life she got around mostly on crutches.

Mrs. Werner was a deeply religious woman who kept her German Bible close at hand and spent much time studying it. About 1960, neighbors and friends bought her a wheelchair to ease her difficulty in getting around.

Eugene married Helenanne Lowe, January 31, 1947. They had one daughter, Kathleen Anne (Keeney). When Kathleen

Anne was small, Eugene moved his family to Seattle. He and Helenanne are living in North Bend, Washington (1980).

Kathleen Anne and her husband have one daughter, Rebecca Anne.

## The Samuel Whealy Family

The Samuel Whealy family moved west from Redwood Falls, Minnesota. For a time they lived at Vader, Washington, then moved to Shaniko. Some of the family lived around there for many years. Mrs. Clara Whealy, of Irish stock, was about five feet tall, weighed eighty pounds, and had a ready wit with the quick temper sometimes found in the Irish. She cooked for threshing crews, living in the cook house. She was one of the best cooks available during harvest.

She and some of her boys lived in the vicinity of Biggs several years before her death in 1939. The Whealy children were Bessie, Nellie, Ralph, Lyle, Ruth, Pat and Clifford.

Bessie married Claud Guyton.

Nellie married Cecil Field, a farmer around Wasco. Their sons were Norman, who became Sherman County Sheriff, and Damon, who went to Spokane.

Ralph lived at Terrebonne, where he died.

Lyle married Lavada, a girl from Mississippi, and lived in Shaniko while he was working as a ranch hand. They moved to Washougal, then Arizona, then back to Terrebonne, Oregon.

Ruth lives at Newport, Washington, north of Spokane. Pat lived in Washougal, Washington. Clifford died when a boy.

## Roy and Ida Baker Wheeler

Roy and Ida Wheeler came to Shaniko from Waitsburg, Washington, to take a homestead on what was known as the

Nellie and Bessie Whealy came to Sherman County with their parents when young girls. Some of the Whealy family lived around Shaniko for many years.

Maxwell place. In 1919 Roy became a partner of Thomas Gavin in the purchase of the Pease & Mays store, making it the "Gavin-Wheeler Company." Mr. Wheeler managed the dry goods department and kept books. Mrs Wheeler worked in the office at times. This was in the days when the store was equipped with the old pull cord for change-making in the bookkeeper's office above the main floor. Late in 1929 they moved to Wenatchee, Washington, then to Spokane.

In June, 1930, Mrs. Wheeler wrote, "I so long for my old and dear friends of the sagebrush country that I feel I must see you all ere long. We miss you all and think of your great kindness to us many, many times." A later letter said, "I do wish we could return to Oregon, anywhere I know, Redmond to Burns; how I long for that high altitude, the sagebrush and magnificent distances; living down in a hole doesn't appeal to me." They never did return.

# John J. Wilson
## 1847-1930

John Wilson was a widower when he arrived in Shaniko with his seven children: Rosetta, Claud, Ollie, Harry, David, Annie, and Amanda. Housing was hard to find, so the children, including little Amanda, were cared for the first winter by someone living at the community of Bourbon in Sherman County. Amanda later recalled that winter as the happiest time of her life.

Rosetta "Rose" or "Rosa" (1872-1964) married William Jasper "Jap" Harris, from Missouri, who homesteaded on land adjacent to the Harry Cook place. Jap Harris died in 1919. Harry Cook bought his land. In her later years, Rose lived in Shaniko in a house south of the water tower. Children of Rose Wilson and Jap Harris were Evelyn, who married Floyd Adams; and Bertha, whose husband Charles W. "Charley" Burg took up a homestead near the Cook place. They lived several years near other members of the family on homesteads. The summer heat, winter cold, and rattlesnakes were too much for them so they moved to Portland where they lived out the rest of their lives in the same house (59 years). Their daughters, Annarose and Helen Marie, married and moved to Sheridan and Auburn, Washington, respectively.

Of Rose and Jap Harris' other children, Arlie "Arlene" married George Fine; Maud married John Smith; William "Bill," born in St. Johns, Multnomah County, went to Shaniko as a teenager; Carrie married Bill Quinn (he had four children, she never had any). Later she married Jesse Helyer of Kent. Frank, eight years younger than Carrie, worked on the CCC as a youth, lived in Shaniko with his mother until her death, did farm work, built fences with Ed Cunion, and now buys and sells horses and cattle, making The Dalles his headquarters.

Claud Wilson, son of John Wilson, was born September 2, 1874, and died April 27, 1936. After proving up on his homestead he bought more land near Bakeoven.

His sister Ollie was born in 1879; she married Everett Higgins. They had daughters Mary, Janie, and Ruth. Ruth married Bill Kramer; Ollie later married John Singer. She died in 1923.

Harry Wilson lived at Newberg, Oregon, David "Dave" also homesteaded at Ridgeway. He and his wife, Cherry, had a son Henry and daughter Elaine. Annie Wilson, twin sister of David, married Crogan Dunning; there were no children.

Amanda "Mandy" lived in Shaniko most of her life. She and her husband, Ebenezer Fine, raised five boys: Myron, Harold, Allen "Dude," Jesse, and Wesley. All lived around Shaniko much of their lives.

# 15

## STATISTICALLY SPEAKING

### Employees of the Railroad Company
### (No records are available, but these are remembered people)

#### *Depot Agents*

E.J. "Jim" Wilson was in Shaniko in 1910. He went on to Prineville. His brother Warren worked in the warehouse, lived in the Fisher house. Daughter Marjorie.

Charley N. Smith, wife Elizabeth, daughters Elizabeth and Dorothy.

Edward "Ed" Feldman, wife Florence, daughters Agnes, Opal, and Norma. He went on to Wasco, Oregon, and finally settled in Hermiston. Proud owner of a Hupmobile car.

L.E. Schueler, wife Lulu. Mrs. Schueler's brother, Lyle Purdin, was freight handler at the depot. Daughter Kathryn.

A.O. Parker, about 1920. Children Paul, Roy, and Clara.

William E. Rhodes about 1927. Wife Nella.

Phillip P. Hite; had no family living in Shaniko.

C.S. Quillan, early 1936.

Leo La Mon, wife Rose. Moved to Umatilla.

#### *Conductors*

Frank Clock, one of the first.

Edgar St. Marie, married to Allie Brazeau's sister.

Charles A. Fisk. The Fisk family lived in Shaniko seven or eight years. His wife, Clara, taught Bible classes, evenings, for high school credit. Their sons, Bill, Ed, George, Clarence, Frank, and Fred, were friends of the Rees boys.

Jessie "Jess" Beardsley, children Loren, Charlotte, Genevieve.

Claud Belts; lived in the Fisher house; daughters Clara, Billie.

Andy Bollens - Stingle - O.C. Eby - Pothour - Vernon Banta - Ernest "Shorty" Lewis.

Arch W. "Bulldog" Nelson, son Billy.

## Engineers and Firemen

Hiram Donley, first engineer on the branch. Family lived in Shaniko. Daughter Madge, son Gordon.

Follett, son Charlie and daughter Josie. They moved to Hillsboro when Elmer Lytle built the P.R. & N. Railroad from Hillsboro to Tillamook.

Otto Hinkle, fireman and engineer. Wife Agnes Schmidt.

Louis Fenton, engineer. Daughter Genevieve. Lived in town four or five years.

Paul Illingworth lived in Shaniko while fireman with Hi Donley. Married Grace Caldwell, sister of M.P. Caldwell. Illingworths had two children, Theo and Eldridge "Stub". Theo eventually worked on steamboats as cook for Western Transportation Company, plying up and down the Columbia and Willamette rivers. Stub Illingworth went to railroading after he was grown and worked for the Union Pacific Line.

Pete Penman, fireman, son Percy. His brother Ernest was night watchman in '22-'23.

Bernard "Barney" Martin. Family lived in Shaniko.

Fred Ross, fireman. Lived in Shaniko five or six years. Son Freddie.

Jim Hayden - M.J. Murphy - "Woody" Woodruff.

## Section Foremen

Charley Spitzer - Jed Davis - Grover Coffman.

At one time there were a number of Chinese section hands, and some Mexican labor was used also.

## Mail Clerks

Howard Weise was mail clerk before World War I. At one time his daughter, Lila, was chosen "Miss Oregon". Wife, Melba.

## Watchmen

Clarence Merchant. Son Lee - Roy Ritter - L.E. Fay - Roy Ohlegschleger.

## State of Oregon Highway Crews

First State Highway Foreman in Shaniko - "Pete" Olsen 1917-1927.
1927 Victor Starling
1929 Ben Allen, who moved from Kent, and went on to Condon.
1931 Charles McCutcheon, who moved from Kent as the sections were
being consolidated.

In 1931 Paul Stoutt came as assistant foreman and part of the crew.
In 1935 Stoutt left to become foreman at Parkdale. James Robertson
took his place.

1943 Charles McCutcheon transferred to Astoria to become bridge tender.
1943 James Robertson became foreman. On his death, Charles Lewis was
foreman. He retired and Glenn Roberts was head man until the station
was split between Moro, Maupin, and Madras.

Some of the men who worked with these foremen:

Reuben Ader
Frank Ballargion
Myron Blades
Albert Bolt
Pat Choin
Lew Delco
George Fine
Bill Garrett
Bob Garrett
Bill Hanks
James F. Hester
Paul Stoutt

Leo Lang
Alex Mathieson (retired and returned
to Scotland)
Bill McKinley
Elgin McKinley
James Pfiefer
Jack Rees (worked on patching)
Jim Rees (crew in the summer)
John Reeder
Vergil Steinmetz
Carl Stratton

## Liquor License Ordinance
## Passed Jan. 25, 1901

1901 J.H. Keeney was the first to receive license $200.00
1902 J.H. Keeney
J.J. Wiley
Silvertooth & Co.
1903 Apr. J.J. Wiley
J.M. Keeney
Wm. Reinehart [Sp. sic.]
Silvertooth & Co.
1903 Nov. F.W. Silvertooth and D.A. Hunt received license for unexpired
time of Bert Magee
1904 Apr. Palmer & Wiley
Reinehart & Co.
Thos. Hennegan
J.M. Keeney

1904 Nov. Dunnigan & Blank allowed to continue business formerly con-
         ducted by Thos. Hennegan
1905 Apr. C.V. Palmer
         Wm. Reinehart
         J.M. Keeney
         J.L. Dunagan
1906 Apr. C.V. Palmer
         Wm. Reinehart
         J.M. Keeney
1906 May Silvertooth & Hunt
1906 Oct. Wm. Reinehart
         Winkleman & O'Regon
1907 May Silvertooth & Hunt
         A.S. Wright
         C.J. Schmidt
         Wm. Reinehart
1908 March Wm. Reinehart
         G.C. Schmidt—License refused and he was instructed to close the
         saloon at once. Fee of $200.00 refunded. Reconsidered at the next
         meeting
1908 May Silvertooth & Browder
         A.S. Wright
1908 Dec. L.T. Winkleman
1909 Jan. F.H. Gardner
         J.M. Keeney
         O'Neil Bros.
         J.F. McGee
1909 Nov. I. Segal
         A.W. Howell
1910 Jan. Stark & Ryder Wholesale liquor license
         Silvertooth & Browder in less than 1 gal.
         Wm. Reinehart in less than 1 gal.
         J.M. Keeney in less than 1 gal.
         O'Neil Bros. in less than 1 gal.
         J.F. McGee in less than 1 gal.
1911 Jan. Wm. Reinehart
1912 J.F. McGee
         C.M. Rosenbaum
1912 Sept. W.H. Nash
1913 Jan. C.M. Rosenbaum
         J.F. Magee
1913 Apr. Sim Browder
1913 July J.H. Coe
1913 Nov. Transferred from Coe to J.F. McGee
         Transferred from Rosenbaum to C.S. Hinton

1915 Sim Browder
   Robertson
   Magee
   [It can be seen that the greatest number of licenses issued in any year was in 1910 when five saloons were selling liquor by the drink. There was one wholesale liquor license that year, in addition to the above mentioned. The often quoted "7 to 17" saloons in Shaniko at a given time is not borne out in record.]

## Excerpts from City Recorders Court

Mar. 4, 1925, 1:35 A.M. "One Robert Burns, drunk, disorderly on vanilla extract arrested by Marshall Bogart. Fined $10.00 on account of his having only $5.00; half of fine suspended on condition he leave the city.

March 10, 1925 5 a.m. Sunday. One Oscar Butler arrested for being drunk and disorderly, confined in City Jail from which he escaped about 11:00 a.m. It is of opinion most everyone, some assistance from outside was given prisoner.

March 10, 1925 The Council met in Special Session. Mayor Gavin presided. Purpose: To investigate Oscar Butlers escape from City while in Jail and who assisted him to escape.

It was moved by Mayor and supported by entire council that such evidence as was in the Councils possession and facts in the case be referred to the Prosecuting Atty. in The Dalles. A. O. Parker, recorder.

## Cemeteries

Inquiries have been received concerning the location of the Shaniko Cemetery. The ground being shallow and rocky, there was never a cemetery for Shaniko, though there were a few scattered graves. In the early days, Shaniko and Bakeoven families buried their dead at what was then known as the "Hinton Cemetery," located a short distance below the house built by R.R. Hinton.

Another burial place soon came into use, also in the Bakeoven area, known as the "Buzan Cemetery," located across the road from the present gate into the Lindley ranch. As soon as travel to The Dalles became convenient, people from Shaniko, Bakeoven and Antelope began burying their dead in the Odd Fellows or Catholic cemeteries there. The following pages list the graves in the two burial grounds mentioned above. A few Shaniko people with Antelope connections were buried at the cemetery in Antelope.

## Buzan Cemetery

This cemetery is located in the Bakeoven area of Wasco County, Oregon. Some refer to it as the Lindley Cemetery. There is evidence of a great deal of work having been done on this cemetery in recent years. Stakes indicate that an effort has been made to plot the area so that graves will be placed in rows.

*Row 1*

| | |
|---|---|
| KRAMER | Maxcine (Maxine is correct spelling) Ruth Kramer<br>Beloved dau. of William and Ruth Kramer<br>1920-1937 |
| SINGER | Ollie Wilson Singer    "Mother"<br>1879-1923<br>Clarence L. Singer<br>Oregon VT 166 Depot Brig.<br>Feb. 11, 1934 |
| HARRIS | William J. Harris<br>1858-1919<br>Rosetta Harris<br>1872-1964    (above 2 on same stone) |
| FINE | Lowel E., son of G.E. & A. Fine<br>March 23, 1919, 4 mo. 23 days |

*Row 2*

| | |
|---|---|
| WILSON | Claud Wilson<br>D. Apr. 27, 1936  61 yrs. 7 mo. 25 days<br>John J. Wilson<br>1847-1930 |
| FINE | Amanda G. Fine<br>1890-1958    (Smith Callaway Chapel) |
| BROWN | James H. Brown<br>July 18, 1876-June 14, 1915  (flag has been placed on grave) |
| HARVEY | George Harvey<br>Died Nov. 25, 1915 aged 75 years 3 mo. 9 days. (flag) |
| WAKERLIG | Maria Wakerlig<br>May 25, 1851-Feb. 29, 1906<br>Rosa Wakerlig<br>Jan. 25, 1884-Nov. 18, 1906 |
| BUTLER | Louise Butler, dau of Mary McKinley<br>Brother Bill Butler Son of Louise |

BLEAKNEY  John G. Bleakney
     May 1, 1832-Nov. 18, 1913
     G.A.R.
     Lewis A. Bleakney   "Father"
     1865-1923
     Minnie M. Bleakney,  "Mother"
     1874-1955
     (Spencer & Libby)
HOLT   James L. Holt
     1879-1953
     (Spencer & Libby)
     Adrian Holt
     1918-1928
NICHOLSON Minnie A. Nicholson
     1854-1943
     (C.R. Callaway & Son)


*Row 3 - No graves listed*

*Row 4*
ASHLEY  Lonnie R. Ashley
     July 20, 1928 Age 11 mo.
     Mattie M. Ashley
     Died May 24, 1964, Aged 80 yrs. 10 mo. 13 das.
BUZAN  Elizabeth L. Buzan
     1919-1932
     Frances, wife of Jerome Buzan
     Jan. 29, 1867-April 5, 1902
     Frances M. Buzan
     1913-1914
     Zella M. Buzan
     1885-
     Frank W. Buzan
     1885-1922
     (Zella M. & Frank W. Buzan on same stone)
LINDLEY  Zelma, wife of A.T. Lindley
     Oct. 2, 1887-Jan. 4, 1928
PURCELL  William Purcell  (no dates)
MITCHEL  Leroy Mitchel
     Died April 28, 1915
     (Age not given)

*Row 5*

PLASTER  Sarah E. Plaster   "Mother"
     Dec. 11, 1856-Mar. 16, 1931

LINDLEY    A.T. Lindley
             Aug.  ,    -Jan. 4,1954
             Melvin W. Lindley
             1915-1943
ANDRUS    Lena Kendrick
             Wife of S.T. Andrus
             Died Apr. 5, 1903 Aged 27 Yrs.

*Row 6*

FLANAGAN  Flanagan Baby   (no dates)
TUNISON    John M. Tunison
             Aug. 5, 1910-Aug. 13, 1910
NORTHRUP  Mrs. D. Northrup
             1832-1909
CROFOOT    Lester E. Crofoot
             May 29, 1925-Jan. 20, 1926
SAYER       Sayer Baby    (no date)
*Row 7*
TUNISON    Barbara J. Tunison
             Metal Marker - (no dates)
WOODS      Harry Woods
             Died Nov. 4, 1932 Age 64 yrs.
TUNISON    Cyrus E. Tunison    "Father"
             1863-1944
             Loretta E. Tunison     "Mother"
             His Wife (Cyrus E.)

             1870-1926 (The above 2 are on the same large stone)

ALDRIDGE  Sarah Aldridge
             Died Mar. 16, 1931 Age 73

## Hinton Cemetery

| | | |
|---|---|---|
| PATJENS | M. Patjens<br>1948 | "Father" |
| | Ernest Patjens<br>Ethel R. Patjens<br>1906-1971 | "Mother" |
| PATJENS | Adele S. Patjens<br>1883-1960 | "Mother" |
| | Andy Patjens<br>1879-1967 | "Father" |
| MEYER | Reimer Meyer<br>1868-1925 | |
| McKINELY | John McKinely<br>1831-1908 | |
| NEWTON | W.I. Newton<br>March 7, 1837-July 20, 1895 | |
| YEAKEY | Ellen Yeakey<br>July 18, 1843-November 12, 1908 | |
| BURKE | George E. Burke<br>May 22, 1872-January 11, 1905 | |
| WOOLSEY | Woolsey<br>1910-1970 | |
| VERMAL | Ellwell E. Vermal<br>1907 | |
| GREGORY | Infant son of T.G. & L. Gregory<br>1904 | |
| JONES | William Jones, son of A.P. & E.L. Jones<br>1892 | |
| | August A. Jones, son of A.P. & E.L. Jones<br>August 4-September 2, 1892 | |
| HINTON | Mary Emma Hinton, wife of R.R. Hinton<br>November 22, 1802-February 9, 1884 | |
| | Mary Ann Bird Hinton, R.R. Hinton's second wife<br>1824-1912 | |
| DAVIS | Oren E. Davis<br>1835-1912 | "Father" |
| | Lydia M. Davis<br>1838-1912 | "Mother" |
| | George Oren Davis, son of James and Erie Davis<br>Died November 2, 1910, 3 months and 14 days | |

# Plat
## of
## Shaniko
## Wasco County
## Oregon

Filed for Record Sept 2d 1899

Seventh     Street

Sixth     Street

Fifth     Street

Fourth     Street

Third     Street

Second     Street

First     Street

Columbia Southern Railway

# Location of Occupants on Plat

The streets east and west were designated by numbers one through seven, and those going north and south by letters A through F. The Columbia Southern Hotel (now Shaniko Hotel) is located on the corner of 4th & E. Few people knew or had reason to care what the streets were named, once the buildings were located. The private dwellings show a succession of occupants. Incomplete lisiting.

| Block | Lot | Occupant |
|---|---|---|
| 1 | 1 | Gregory, Ed Henton, Whealy, Gott |
| 2 | 6 | Fenton, Cole Smith, Tommy Jones |
| 2 | 7-8-9 | School House |
| 3 | 1 | Esping, Mike Reeder, Mary Rice |
| 3 | 3 | Fowlie, Logan, Casebolt |
| 3 | 7 | Werner |
| 4 | 3 | Spear, Fisk, Robertson |
| 4 | 5 | Schmidt, Hill, Wheeler |
| 4 | 6 | Water Tower |
| 5 | | |
| 6 | | |
| 7 | 2 | Bentley, Altermatt, Harris, Julie Robeson |
| 7 | 3 | Reeder, Al. Jones, T. Jones, Claud Guyton |
| 8 | 1-2 | First School Bldg. |
| 8 | 3-4 | Esping, Fine, Wilson, Elizabeth Spires |
| 8 | 5-6 | Wornstaff |
| 9 | 1 | Hoech, Altermatt, Wagner, Jim Robertson, Alice Roberts, Cora Willich |
| 9 | 2-3 | Moody, Adelbert Rees, Hanks, Lloyd Harold |
| 9 | 4-5 | Claud Belts, J.W. Fisher, Ed Cunion |
| 10 | 5-6 | Townsite Bldg. |
| 10 | 7-8 | Owl Roost, Sherman Restaurant, Millie Pullen-Dance Hall, Wayne McCulloch, Garage, Glade's Restaurant and Shell Station |
| 10 | 9 | Moody Garage |
| 10 | 11-12 | Jas. McHargue, A.H. Pratt, John McHargue, Adelbert Rees. Ivan Olsen moved house to Madras |
| 11 | 1-2-3-4-10-11-12 | W.A. Rees, John R. Rees, present owner |
| 11 | 4 | Reams |
| 11 | 5 | Cornett Family |
| 11 | 6 | Cornett Stage and Dickey Restaurant |
| 11 | 7-8 | Pease & Mays Store, Silvertooth & Browder Saloon, Alex Ross Garage and residence, W.H. Johnson, Morelli's Wagon Yard |
| 11 | 9 | City Hall |
| 12 | 1-2-3 | Camp Cabins, Dance Hall |
| 12 | 3 | John Reid, John Joyce |
| 12 | 4-5-6 | Columbia Southern Hotel |
| 12 | 8 | Gus Reeder's Harness Shop, City Garage, Austin Brazeau. Allie Brazeau ran the store and pool hall. |
| 13 | 1-2-3 | Apartments - long, like the Owl Roost. Houses of F.T. Esping, Peterkin, Appling, Butcher, Selma Johnson (teacher) in front shop. Esther, Arnie Christiansen and Lizzie Esping. |
| 13 | 4-5 | Rosa Harris |
| 14 | 1 | |
| 14 | 2 | Gus Reeder, Claud Guyton, Elgin McKinley (?) (?) (?) (?) |
| 14 | 3 | |
| 14 | 4 | Lane, Uren, Gus Reeder, Claud Guyton, Bonney, Adelbert Rees, Ivan Olsen moved the house to Madras |
| 14 | 5 | (?) |
| 14 | 6 | Reeder, Claud Guyton |
| 14 | 7-8 | Feed Barn, Dell Howell |
| 14 | 9 | Delbert Wolfe, Clyde Bonney (?) (?), Allie Brazeau |
| 14 | 10 | Berglund, Bill Kramer, Donley, Widener |
| 14 | 11 | Kinney, Rosenbaum, Dell Howell's home, Pete Olsen |
| 15 | | (?)----- |
| 16 | 1-2-3 4-5-6 to 12 | Feed Lot |
| 17 | 1-2 | Blacksmith Shop, Ben Herring |
| 17 | 3 | (?) (?) (?) (?) (?) Will Guyton (?) (?) |
| 17 | 4 | (?) |
| 17 | 5 | Plaster |
| 17 | 6 | Davis, Sumner, T. Jones, Salnave |
| 18 | | Pease & Mays Store (Gavin-Wheeler, then Ivan Olsen's Shaniko Store) Pat & Bill's Texaco Station & P.O., Leo Butcher's Texaco |
| 18 | 3-4 | Vacant (?) Tennis Court |
| 18 | 5-6 | Wheeler |
| 18 | 7-8 | |
| 19 | 1 | Sanford's Store, Drugstore run by Doc Wilson |
| 19 | 5 | Eagle Hotel, Jewelry Store, Bakery, Bowling Alley, Al Howell's Saloon where the big fire started. |
| 19 | 10 | Gus Reeder's Harness Shop |
| 20 | 1-2 | Feed Barn, (?) (?) |
| 20 | 11 | Bank, Reinhart, Mrs. James Robertson and son Pete, Bill Gott |
| 20 | 12 | Reinhart Saloon, Robertson Saloon, Robertson Livery Barn |
| 21 | 9 | Harness Shop |
| 21 | 10-11-12 | Hotel Shaniko |
| 22 | 1 | Minnie Bleakney |
| 22 | 2-3-4-5-6-7-8 | (?) |
| 22 | 10 | Big Community Hall |
| 23 | 1 | (?) |
| 23 | 3 | Wiley home |
| 23 | 4-5-6 | (?) |
| 23 | 7 | (?) |
| 23 | 9 | Drug Store |
| 23 | 11-12 | Blondon, Overman, R.I. Kinney, (?) (?), Mrs. Garrett, (?) (?) |

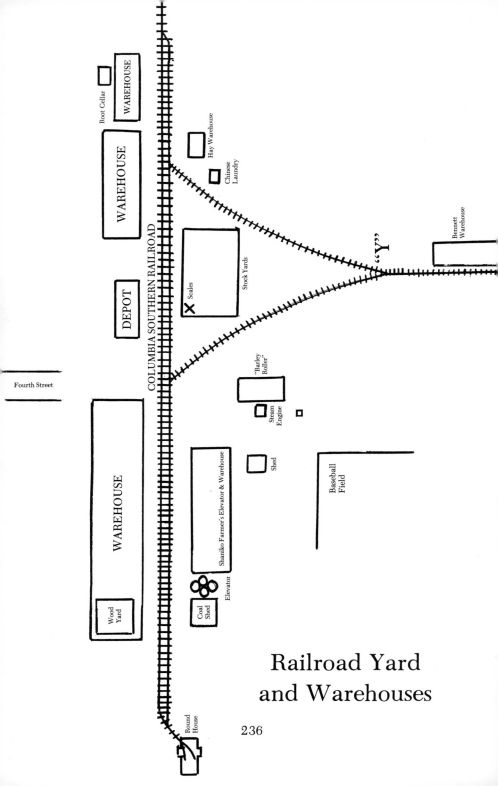

Railroad Yard
and Warehouses

236

# INDEX

## A

Abendechein, Kevin, 172
Ackerman, Maria, 117
Adams, John Family, 114; Bertha,
114; Connie, 115; Floyd, 223;
Leland, 114; Mary, 115; Olive
"Ollie", 114; Oscar, 114, 115;
Pearl, 116
Alden, Mrs., 7
Aldrich, Sarah, 232
Allen, Ben, 227
Altermatt, Archer R. Family, 116;
Alphons, 118; Archer, 114, 116,
117, 118, 150, 153, 180; Darrel,
97, 105, 116, 117, 153; Dorothea,
118; Gertrude, 118; John, 118;
John Baptist, 117; Karl von
Ramiswil, 117; Louise Mildred,
35, 116, 117; Martha Mabel, 118,
180; Nelson, 118; Pius Fredrick,
118; Robert, 116, 153; Sidney, 118
Amiens, 76
Armstrong, Leonard, 73, 75
Arnold, A.N., 32
Ashby, W.J., 9
Asher, Matt, 120
Ashley, Thelma, 129

## B

Bade, Elizabeth, 178
Baird, Nathan, 9
Bales, Harriet, 32
Bamer, Mary Maggie, 15
Barlow, Mrs. Frank, 141
Barr, Lola, 32
Bayer, Charlotte, 225; Claud, 181;
Jess, 225; Loren, 225
Bell, Ada, 2, 3, 5, 6, 20, 69
Bellargion, Frank, 227
Belts, Clara, 225; Claud, 225
Bennett, J.T., 10
Bentley, Blanche, 4; Madge, 26, 27
Bergstrom, William Lewis, 159
Beyer, Walter, 216
Bichsell, Velma, 32
Biedron, Helen Juliana, and John, 205
Bird, Jim, 75; Mary Ann, 91
Blades, Clara, 126; Myron, 227
Bleakney, Alice (Brown) and Darrel

Alvin, 174; Ethel, 173; Evelyn,
174; John, 173, 231
Bleakney, Lg, 173, 174, 184; Lewis,
231; Louis, 173; Marjorie, 174;
Mattie, 174; Minnie, 230; Tenny,
173; Theodore "Teddy", 173
Blondin, F.A., 21
Blossick, Tom, 153
Blueline, 142
Bogart Family, 127, 153
Eugene L., 21, 73, 77, 229
Bollens, Andy, 104, 225
Bolt, Albert, 227
Bolter, Eva and Twins, 35; Lila, 35
Bolton, Edna, 35
Bolton Mercantile Co., 9, 21, 23
Bonney Family, 118, 120, 201
Bonney, Augustus A., 118; Clyde T.,
32, 119; Margaret, 118; Martha,
35; Rex and Thelma, 118
Bordwell, Ed, 184
Borthwick Family, 120; Barbara,
Billie, Eldon, 36, 120; Janet, 36,
120; Lottie, 35, 36
Bowen, Gus, 160
Bower, Fred "Bud", 185
Boyce, A.W., 58, 60, 61, 62
Brazeau, Allie, 119, 225; Austin, 76;
Giles, 76
Broughton, L.V., 32
Browder, Sim, 229
Brown, Alice Lenora, 173
Brown, Andrew J. and Alida, 120
Anna May (Fine) and Adeline, 120
Jean (Ingram) Gabel, 120
Brown, Bullfrog, 67
Brown, Clifford, 119
Brown, Walter Family, 120
James L., 125, 230
Brown's, 157
Brown, Walter Bullard, 88, 120, 173
Brownhill, Ada, 35
Brumbaugh, Frank, 31
Bruner, Ferdinand H. Family, 121;
Abigail, Don, Elinor Melda, 121;
Ferdinand "Farnim", Henry, 121;
Herb, Ivan Raymond, 121; Melda,
121, 122; Oliver Wayne, Ruth
Genevieve, 121
Buchanan, Capt. A., 38
Burg, Charles Family, 223

*Shaniko People*

Jessie, 223; Myrtle, Norma Jean, 115; Ollie, Virginia, 115
Hennegan, Thomas, 227, 228
Henry the Cop, 172
Henry, Thomas, 168, 169
Hetleslater, Jennie (Maywood, Coffee), 32
Hewett "The Great", Bessie, 24
Higgins, Everett, Janie, Mary, Ruth, 224
Hill, Frank N., 12; Frank, 12, 18; Grace, 14; Harry, 3, 12, 14, 15, 18, 19; Mrs., 18; Wayne, 67
Hinkle, Agnes, Dorothy, Ernest, 215; Otto, 226
Hinton Cemetery, 229, 233
Hinton, Family, 148; C.S., 228; James E. "Jim", 184, 220; Mary Ann (Bird), 93, 233; Mary Emma, 223; Mary Loula "Mary Lou", 91, 92, 148; Minnie, 92, 94, 147; Ranch, 126; Richard "Dickie", 91, 92, 95, 147; Richard Roland "RR", 75, 85, 91, 95, 147, 229; Robert "Bobby", 92, 93, 147, 148
Hoech Family, 121, 149, 150; Irene, 137, 150; Irma, 137, 150; J.W., 141; Lulu, 141
Holder, William, 23
Holt, Adrian, 174, 175, 231; Alma, 174; Andrew "Andy", 113, 151; Bill, Frank, 174; Lester "Les", 106, 172, 174, 175; James L., 231; Mabel, 116; Millie, 172; Minnie, 172, 173; Phoebe (Robertson), 151
Hood, Janice, 181; Joe, Michael, Ronald, 181
Hopkins, Jessie C., 90
Horton, Mrs. Ray, 218
Hougan, Alma, 35
Howell, A.W., 228; Dellmar A., 24; Livery Stable, 4, 18, 150
Hunt, D.A., 227; Genevieve, 119
Hurlburt, Mayor Frank, 12

### I

Illingworth, Eldridge, 226; Nona, 122; Paul, 226; Theo, 104, 226
Ingram, Edward, 120; Jan, 120
Indians, Warm Springs, 106
Inman, Millie, 172
Irvine, Frank, 9

### J

Jackson, Alma, 202; Lou, 65; Maxine, 202; Roland D., 202
Jade, Charlotte, 178
Johnson, Bill, 5; Eunice May, 31, 32; Gerald, 27; Lyle, 172; Homestead, 148; Mrs. Selma, 32
Jones, 76; August A., son of AP & EL, 233; Al, 181; Elizabeth, 118; Doris, John Thomas, 11, 181; J.T. "Tommy", 76, 181, 182, 217; J.W., 23; Kelsay, 130; Theresa, 181; William, son of AP & EL, 233
Jordan, Dick, 184
Joyce, "Little John", 160, 162
Joynt, Maud, 32

### K

Karlen, John, 73, 75
Kaseberg, 155
Kaser, Agnes, 214
Keeney, Elias, 151, 157; Ilene, 189; James H., 113, 151, 227; James M., 157, 228; John, 146; Jonathan, 157; Mary Emma, 157, 189
Kellam, Marguerite, 27
Kelly, Anna, 25, 27, 32
Kennedy, Eleanor, 35; Sybil, 35
Kentner, Archibald, 159
Ida Lee, Mabel Frances, 159
Miles Arch, Theodore Wilbur, 159
Kidder, Ira, 119
Kimsey, Belle, 35; Dolph D., 67, 118; Margaret, 35
Kinney Family, 151; Essie, 152; Ethel, 153, 154; Richard I. "Dick", 6, 21, 50, 152, 153, 154
Kircheiner, Peter A., 9
Knudson, Alfred, 126
Kramer Family, 154; Allen "Buddy", 155; Anna, 154, 155; Ed, 154; Ernest "Ernie", 154, 156; Harold, 156; Henry, 154; Joe, 154, 155; Ruth, 155, 230; Sylvester "Vesty", 154, 156; Veronica, 154, 156; William "Bill", 154, 155, 230
Kyllonen, Maye, 204

### L

Lally, John, 126
Lamborn, Frank, 27

# THE AUTHOR

Helen Guyton Rees, born on a farm in 1910, just 10 miles north of Shaniko of homesteader parents, grew up with a large family of relatives and friends coming to visit; therefore, welcoming friends and visitors to the Rees home has been a natural way of life to her.

One of her early memories is hearing her grandfather Guyton point to the bleached ox skull lying by the gate and explaining that many such oxen skulls were seen by his wife Ellen Smith, then 16 years old, as she came along the Oregon Trail from Iowa in a wagon train in 1865. Another memory was hearing her mother, Ada Bell Guyton, say, "We laughed when Papa said we were descended from Pocahontas, until a relative came from the East to visit and said, 'Don't laugh, it's true!' " This remark eventually led the author to an interest in genealogy which has expanded into travel across the United States, tracing ancestors, and of course, looking for evidence of the story about Pocahontas along the way.

Her lifelong interest in history has led her to research and, since 1976, work to finish the history of Shaniko. The Rees family began its life in Shaniko in 1903, when Bill and Lillie Rees were married, and continued until their death.

Adelbert and Helen made Shaniko their home from 1929-1942, and have kept in constant personal contact with relatives and friends ever since. Their four children, now all grown, were born while they lived in Shaniko: Bill, (the Rev. Wm. R. Rees); Richard Harry; Anna Bell, (Mrs. Hal Rosene); and Charles Arthur.

Adelbert and Helen Rees now live in Fairview, Oregon; both are retired from the United States Postal Service.

Mrs. Rees writes on the dining room table, surrounded by the reference materials, letters, pictures, and diaries she has accumulated during her work on Shaniko history. She also has many other interests, including leadership in church affairs, selling imported hand-crafted articles from underdeveloped countries, and keeping close family ties.